To Roger

with much love from Kath

X   Christmas 2003   X

D1389711

Armenia

Armenia

PORTRAITS OF SURVIVAL AND HOPE

Donald E. Miller
Lorna Touryan Miller

Photographs by Jerry Berndt

University of California Press ı Berkeley ı Los Angeles ı London

University of California Press
Berkeley and Los Angeles, California

University of California Press, Ltd.
London, England

© 2003 by the Regents of the University of California

Library of Congress Cataloging-in-Publication Data

Miller, Donald E. (Donald Earl), 1946–
   Armenia : portraits of survival and hope /
Donald E. Miller, Lorna Touryan Miller ; photographs by Jerry Berndt.
     p.   cm.
   Includes bibliographical references and index.
   ISBN 0-520-23492-8
   1. Armenia (Republic)—History—1920–1991.
2. Armenia (Republic)—History—1991–.
3. Nagorno–Karabakh Conflict, 1988–1994.
4. Armenians—Azerbaijan. I. Miller, Lorna
Touryan. II. Berndt, Jerry. III. Title.

  DK687.M59   2003
  947.56'08—dc21   2003000596

Manufactured in the United States of America

12   11   10   09   08   07   06   05   04   03
10   9   8   7   6   5   4   3   2   1

The paper used in this publication meets the minimum
requirements of ANSI/NISO Z39.48–1992 (R 1997)
(Permanence of Paper).⊚

To our two children,
Shont and Arpi

Contents

Acknowledgments

We had just finished writing *Survivors: An Oral History of the Armenian Genocide* when we received a telephone call from Steve Ferguson, a program officer with Fieldstead and Company. He asked us if we would like to expand our research into the contemporary period of Armenian history. The Republic of Armenia had become independent of the former Soviet Union in 1991 and was facing enormous political and economic challenges. Ferguson's employers, Howard and Roberta Ahmanson, were aware of the humanitarian work of Baroness Caroline Cox, a member of British Parliament who had made numerous trips to Armenia and Nagorno-Karabakh, and they were interested in funding a research project that would document the struggle for survival by this Christian nation.

Lorna and I assumed that when *Survivors* was completed, we would move on to other work more closely aligned with our day-to-day jobs. I had just begun a large research project on rapidly growing nonmainline churches, and Lorna was launching a major health-care project for children in Pasadena; it scarcely seemed like a good time to take on another major responsibility—especially one that would involve repeated trips to a country fifteen thousand miles away. Nevertheless, the project was compelling. Armenia was front-page news. First there had appeared devastating photographs of the 1988 earthquake, followed by photographs of hundreds of thousands of people demonstrating for independence, and then accounts of people freezing during the winter because of the blockade imposed by Turkey and Azerbaijan.

On November 25, 1992, we submitted a proposal to the Ahmansons, acknowledging a moral imperative to respond to the crises confronting Armenia. On April 27, 1993, we were officially funded, with the Armenian Missionary Association of America (AMAA) serving as fiscal agent for the project. During the next two years we traveled frequently to Armenia, and when we were not there we stayed in contact with our research team by fax, phone, and e-mail. This research period was followed by an equally intense period during which we mounted the photography exhibit "Armenia: Portraits of Survival," spoke to many audiences about the conditions in Armenia, and worked with our colleagues translating and coding interviews so that this book could be written.

In May 1993, we went to Armenia and hired a ten-member research team, which included eight graduate students who had just completed an English language course at Haigazian College in Yerevan: Alvard Asatrian, Armine Avakian, Nora Ashofi Davidian, Naire Ghairtandjian, Theresa Hakopian, Armine Hovannesian, Ruben Krikorian, and Gayane Yepiskopsian. In addition, Taline Satamian joined the team as a project consultant, and Korioun Alavardian was hired as the project facilitator and logistics manager. Louis Volpp, president of Haigazian College, and his wife, Holly, nurtured the team. Kennel Touryan, associate executive director of the AMAA, also provided valuable moral support for the project, as did Levon Bardakjian, then working for the AMAA.

During our various trips to Armenia, many people were enormously helpful. We would especially like to thank Charlie Hachadourian and his wife, Marineh Fstkchyan. Marineh interviewed refugee children in her school, and Charlie introduced us to the art community in Armenia. He would later become the curator of *Armenia: Portraits of Survival,* an exhibition presented in a number of American cities before traveling to Yerevan in 1998. We also have fond memories of our driver in Armenia, Smpat, as well as the women who managed the fifth floor of the Hotel Armenia. On several trips we were joined by John and Arpi Haleblian, who were a great source of companionship—especially when we visited the soup kitchens and schools that they help support through Bay Area

Friends of Armenia (BAFA). Arpi Haleblian later spent hundreds of hours translating our interviews, which was a heroic undertaking for which we are most grateful. Indeed, the project could not have moved forward without her. And John was a faithful reader of several drafts of this manuscript.

There are also many people to thank here on the home front. Diane Balabanian, then a student at the University of Southern California, translated and transcribed all the interviews that were conducted in Russian. Angie Martinez transcribed almost three hundred interviews. Our daughter, Arpi Miller, a doctoral student in sociology at UCLA, coded all the interviews using the QSR program NUD*IST, a step that greatly facilitated our writing. Margi Denton, of Denton Design, became a wonderful friend during the process of putting together the catalog for the exhibition. Rouben Adalian and Sonia Messirian Crow, who were working with the Armenian Assembly, were unusually helpful with the exhibition, as well as with distribution of the catalog to members of Congress and heads of nongovernmental organizations. Rita Balian heroically organized the exhibition opening in the rotunda of the Senate Office Building in Washington, D.C. And Richard Hovannisian, a constant source of intellectual support throughout our Armenian-related historical research, offered invaluable comments on this manuscript.

Our closest companion in this project, however, has been Jerry Berndt. We have spent hundreds of hours together traveling and sharing meals, editing contact sheets, and speaking at exhibitions. Through the lens of his camera we have seen the people of Armenia in a new way. More recently, in his new work on religion and immigration in Los Angeles, we have come to view our own city from a different perspective thanks to his artistic eye. Indeed, whatever shortcoming the text of this book may have, the photographs tell their own story of survival and hope.

We also acknowledge the reporting of Armenia International Magazine (AIM), the Armenian General Benevolent Union's news magazine, the daily listserv of Armenian news, GROONG, hosted by the University of Southern California, and the numerous Internet sites sponsored by various Armenian organizations.

Finally, we thank the three hundred people who shared their stories with us. Our only regret is that we cannot hear from them again, in this new century, to find out how their lives have changed and to see their dreams realized and their commitment to survival honored.

Armenia and Azerbaijan

Introduction

Setting Up Shop in Yerevan

We struggled to lift our carry-on bags into the overhead bin of the KLM flight taking us to Paris. Inside were ten tape recorders, several transcribing machines, batteries, and much of the apparatus required to set up a research office in Yerevan, Armenia. Our checked luggage contained a small gasoline-powered electric generator and a thousand cassette tapes, not to mention clothes, a laptop computer, and gifts—inexpensive calculators and quarter-pound bags of coffee intended for the people we would interview.

Any anxiety we had about imperiling passengers with our heavy suitcases was laid to rest when we left Paris on a Russian-built Armenia Airlines plane. People were smoking during takeoff, and the stewardesses were walking around as the plane taxied down the runway. The seatbelts seemed to be at least as old as the carpet in the aisles, which was rumpled and worn. But whatever the plane lacked in style was balanced by the class of passengers, among whom were the conductor of Armenia's philharmonic orchestra, the head of the energy department of Armenia, the president of the American University of Armenia, a member of British Parliament, and a future foreign minister of Armenia and his family, as well as physicists, engineers, businessmen, and representatives of several nongovernmental organizations (NGOs).

Within twenty-four hours of our arrival in the Republic of Armenia, we had met the president of Haigazian College and were interviewing graduate students in the school's MBA program—potential research assistants who would help us document the social and economic conditions in post-Soviet Armenia. We offered them thirty dollars a month—double the salary of professors in nearby Yerevan State University, though in effect a bare subsistence wage. We hired a logistics coordinator to arrange travel, manage the office, and serve as the financial liaison with Haigazian College. We also hired a graduate of the University of California at Los Angeles who had been living in Armenia and had experience conducting oral history interviews.

The next two years were a research adventure, as well as some of the saddest days of our lives. We traveled regularly to Armenia to monitor the research, which was focused on four populations: (1) survivors of the earthquake that devastated northwestern Armenia in 1988; (2) refugees from Azerbaijan who fled the cities of Sumgait and Baku because of pogroms; (3) women, children, and soldiers affected by the war in Nagorno-Karabakh; and (4) ordinary citizens who had survived several winters without heat because of the blockade imposed by Turkey and Azerbaijan.

At the end of two years we had more than 300 tape-recorded interviews. Eventually 289 of these were translated, transcribed, and coded, yielding thousands of pages of testimony about the social, economic, and spiritual condition of Armenians in 1993 and 1994, several years after the Republic of Armenia declared independence from the former Soviet Union on September 23, 1991.

In addition to conducting interviews in and around Yerevan, the capital of Armenia, our research team traveled to the earthquake-damaged areas of Spitak and Gyumri (formerly Leninakan), as well as Stepanakert, the capital of the Nagorno-Karabakh enclave. Also, a small subset of the research team went to Moscow and interviewed people who had left Armenia to look for employment. We traveled with the team to all of these locations except for Moscow, but for the most part, the team worked on its own, and we kept in touch with them by e-mail and telephone.

Photojournalist Jerry Berndt accompanied us on our second trip to Armenia. He had experience in Cuba, the dance studios of Boston, and the halls of corporate business. This connection was fortuitous, but also seemed divinely ordained, because in response to our original grant proposal, the foundation deemed our methodology well designed but wondered how we would communicate the Armenian tragedy to the American public and to policymakers. Asked to consider adding a visual dimension to the project, we called Jerry, whom we had met briefly while he was on an assignment in Los Angeles. "How would you like to go to Yerevan?" we asked. Rather than negotiate a fee, or ask, "Why?" or "Where is Yerevan?" his immediate response was, "Sure, when do we leave?"

During the three weeks we spent together in August 1993, we learned more about photography than Jerry learned about sociological research methods. We had assumed that we would chauffeur Jerry around from site to site, that he would snap a few pictures, and then we would be on our way. We did not know that it was important for him to linger over coffee or share a bottle of vodka with our subjects and wait until his camera became invisible before it even came out of his bag. Neither did we anticipate the formidable process of editing contact sheets, setting up an exhibition, and arranging for its travel—because travel it did, from Los Angeles to New York, Boston, Washington, D.C., and then to Fresno, Pasadena, Glendale, and, eventually, Yerevan.

Fortunately, we engaged a good curator, Charles Hachadourian, but we also traveled to the opening of each exhibit, prepared speeches, and worked with a designer who put together a powerful presentation of the photographs in a booklet that we called "Armenia: Portraits of Survival." This was mailed to every member of the United States Congress and to newspapers, academics, and heads of NGOs. For a while, our living room floor looked like a mass-mail sorting room, as we addressed envelopes and affixed stamps. Needless to say, this did not feel like a typical academic research project.

We also had our moments of crisis. One night we were awakened by Jerry knocking on the door of our room in the Hotel Armenia and saying, "I need a doctor." He was suffering from either appendicitis or a kidney stone. Not knowing what to do, we started pounding on hallway doors, looking for a group of physicians from Cyprus who were traveling to Nagorno-Karabakh. Finally we located a doctor, only to be told that his medical bag was held up in customs. So we decided to wait out the night. By early morning we learned that Jerry was, indeed, passing a kidney stone, and we lost only one day of work. Experiences such as this one did not stop Jerry, who would later return to Armenia in the dead of winter to document everyday life in Yerevan.

The Research Experience

Although the last interview took place in 1994, five years passed before we could begin writing. During this time, Arpi Haleblian translated the Armenian interviews, which were then transcribed. Our daughter, Arpi Miller, helped us code the interviews into several hundred thematic categories. Meanwhile we were also busy at our jobs, Don as a professor at the University of Southern California and Lorna as director of the Office for Creative Connections at All Saints Church in Pasadena.

During much of this time we had lingering feelings of guilt, because we had been entrusted with so much by the people we and our research team had interviewed. When was the book going to get written? At last, during a sabbatical leave in the fall of 2000, Don turned his attention to the hundreds of pages of transcripts and coded interviews and began writing. We felt an urgent desire to finish this book before the tenth anniversary of the rebirth of the Republic of Armenia.

Our thinking had matured during this hiatus, and as a result this book is not simply about a crisis to which the world is called to respond. More profound issues arose while we worked our way slowly through the raw data. Present in these interviews were the deepest expressions of the human spirit. When the physical and social structures of a society are tested to their limits, profound insights emerge from the ways people make meaning in the face of adversity.

Humanistic scholars often note that individual experience sheds light on universal truths. Indeed, these interviews communicate profound truths as they reveal the role of self-sacrifice and neighborly love in sustaining community, the need for vision and belief in the future in order to overcome hopelessness and despair, the importance of commemorating the dead as well as celebrating rites of passage for the living, and the status of political ideals—freedom, independence, self-determination—as the foundation of life and meaning. Consequently, this book is more than a story about how the Armenians struggled in the face of political persecution and natural disaster. It is an invitation to embrace the spirit of compassion, to think beyond an insular worldview, and to give thanks for the basic human necessities of food, warmth, shelter, freedom, and peace.

One of our greatest fears is that those of us who enjoy these privileges have developed compassion fatigue. While we often respond heroically to crises, once the bandage has been applied, we are tempted to turn the page and wait for the next story that grabs our attention or, on another level, serves our national self-interest. The bubble of affluence in which most of us live—in which we take for granted running water, grocery stores stocked with food, and thermostats we can turn up or down at will—insulates us from the reality of at least a third of our fellow human beings on this globe.

Nor can most of us imagine having to cope with archaic bureaucracies that impose self-serving rules and other impediments to efficiency and free market exchange—in the case of Armenia, the legacy of seventy years of communism. A large number of people, including many diaspora Armenians who invested in the economy of the new republic, came away frustrated, convinced that their efforts were not worth the trouble. More than once we heard the following sentiment: "If they don't want our money and expertise, there are plenty of people who do."

The first time we visited Armenia was in 1990, when the spirit of democracy was vibrant. We were there just after a million people demonstrated in support of independence and the unification of Nagorno-Karabakh with Armenia. As guests of the government, we were wined and dined as part of a symposium on the Armenian genocide. We sampled a dozen different vintages of brandy at the local factory and heard at least as many toasts to our health, to the health of our children, and to the freedom of Armenia. But in 1993, when this research project was born, people were barely thawing out from an exceptionally harsh winter. Many had died from the cold, and some people we spoke to reported having lost ten or fifteen pounds. Surviving on half a pound of bread a day is not easy. The schools had been closed for the winter, because there was no fuel to heat them. When we returned to our home in Pasadena and walked into a grocery store loaded not only with food but also with multiple brands of every conceivable item, we experienced a form of culture shock. We were overwhelmed by the inequalities that exist in this world.

American culture boasts of happy endings, and Americans are the first to argue for hope and transformation. But the mood is not so bright in Armenia, which has been plagued by violence. Fortunately, the 1994 cease-fire in Nagorno-Karabakh is still in effect as we write. The nuclear plant in Medzamor has been reactivated, and most people have electricity (those who can pay for it; utilities are now privatized). For those with money, there is food to buy on the grocery shelves. On the other hand, when we recently visited soup kitchens, we found that, in addition to the elderly, children were coming to eat and to bring food back to their families. Half the population is barely subsisting, and people are begging on the streets—something one never saw before independence. The schools we visited in villages on the periphery of the earthquake zone, as well as some near the Azerbaijani border, were a travesty, especially considering that Armenia was formerly reputed to have a higher percentage of people with doctoral degrees than any other country in the world. It touched our hearts to be served coffee in broken cups by the school principals, knowing that they were offering their best. After we walked through schools housed in temporary post-earthquake structures, riddled with shrapnel and shell holes and lacking desks to accommodate all the students, we considered the sorry state of schools in Los Angeles from a very different perspective.

On the surface, things were better during our last visit, in 2001, ten years after Armenia declared independence. But we are saddened by the fact that a third or more of Armenia's three and a half million people have emigrated, which has resulted in a substantial brain drain. Many elderly are in desperate straits, their pensions nearly worthless. And more than half of the population is unemployed or severely underemployed. People are directing misplaced anger at each other, partly because government structures are failing to meet their needs. Furthermore, many people seem to be on the verge of giving up hope, at least in terms of the present. If they have hope, it is for their children, not for themselves. Individuals speak of how established networks of family and community are breaking down. Because so many died in the war and hundreds of thousands have emigrated, the social networks—what sociologists call "social capital"—are threatened, and these are the bedrock of any healthy democracy.

The Historical Context

Armenians bring a unique context to their struggle for liberation. In 1915 half of the Armenian population living in Ottoman Turkey was annihilated through genocidal death marches and massacres. These were preceded by pogroms that killed at least a hundred thousand people in 1895 and 1896 and another thirty thousand in 1909. When politicians carved up territory after World War I, Armenia not only lost its western provinces to Turkey, it also lost Nakhichevan, on its southern border, and Nagorno-Karabakh. Almost 90 percent of the territory that was once historic Armenia is occupied by other countries, leaving to present-day Armenia a tiny area about the size of Maryland—one that is scarcely viable, with few natural resources and no seaport, and culturally isolated, with Muslim neighbors on three sides.

Armenia was the first nation to convert to Christianity, early in the fourth century, and religion has played an important role in maintaining national identity. It has also distinguished Armenians as a minority population within a largely Islamic region of the world. While not the primary basis for the genocide of 1915, religion was a factor, because it had kept Armenians from assimilating with their Turkish neighbors. Intermarriage, for example, was extremely rare. Moreover, religion connected Armenians to the predominantly Christian societies of Western Europe and the United States, under whose influence Armenians modernized more rapidly than their Turkish neighbors. While jealousy may have helped motivate the extermination of Armenians, a more important motive was a racist nationalist ideology that gripped the leaders of the Young Turk movement, who saw Armenians as not only a potential threat but also an impediment to creating an empire that would unite all Turkic peoples from Constantinople (Istanbul) to central Asia.

After World War I, Armenia existed as an independent republic for only two years, from 1918 to 1920. Then Mustafa Kemal, the self-proclaimed president and prime minister of Turkey, squashed the fledgling, desperately poor country, and what was left of Armenia was placed under Soviet control. In 1921 Nagorno-Karabakh, at that time 95 percent Armenian, was made an autonomous *oblast* (district) under Soviet Azerbaijan, and Nakhichevan, which was 40 percent Armenian, was also put under Azerbaijani governance. Nakhichevan was eventually emptied of its Armenian population, and by 1979 the population of Nagorno-Karabakh had become 75 percent Armenian. In 1987 and 1988 there were mass demonstrations of Armenians favoring unification with Nagorno-Karabakh, followed by pogroms against Armenians living in Azerbaijan. The spirit of the Nagorno-Karabakh Armenians was not diminished, however, and in July 1988 the Nagorno-Karabakh Soviet voted to secede unilaterally from Azerbaijan.

A severe earthquake hit northwestern Armenia on December 7, 1988. The news was greeted in Azerbaijan by cheers in student dormitories and celebration in the streets. Armenians living in Azerbaijan continued to be harassed as the conflict with Nagorno-Karabakh intensified, and there were renewed pogroms against Armenians in Baku, the capital city of Azerbaijan, in 1989 and 1990. Already burdened with taking care of a half million homeless earthquake survivors, Armenia had to absorb approximately two hundred thousand Armenian refugees from Azerbaijan.

By the time Armenia became independent in 1991, Turkey and Azerbaijan had imposed a blockade on the tiny, landlocked nation, which not only put a complete chokehold on the economy but also created great obstacles to the entry of foreign aid. And because the nuclear power plant in Armenia had been shut down after the earthquake for fear of a Chernobyl-like accident, the country was cast into near darkness, with one or two hours of electricity a day, and sometimes not even that much. The only fuel coming into Armenia came through Georgia, where pipelines were sabotaged by Turks loyal to Azerbaijan.

To those outside Armenia, it might seem absurd for Armenian citizens to maintain their commitment to the Nagorno-Karabakh cause, given the incredible demands placed on them by the earthquake, the refugees from Azerbaijan, and the blockade. We need, therefore, to understand the national psyche, which was deeply affected by the loss of half of the population in 1915, the elimination of Armenians from eastern Turkey and Nakhichevan, and the pogroms against fellow Armenians—many of whom had lost the use of their mother tongue—in Azerbaijan. All it took to release the expression of strong nationalistic feelings was for Gorbachev to promulgate his twin doctrines of glasnost and perestroika. In both Armenia and Nagorno-Karabakh, Armenians felt that they were simply expressing the right to criticism and self-determination that was provided for under the Soviet constitution.

The Perspective of Oral History

Historical books often focus on the personalities and decisions of the leaders of nations and the geopolitics of the social and economic context that gives rise to wars, treaties, and cultural advancement. This book assumes a different perspective, focusing on the experiences of common people—their perceptions, their viewpoints. Our intention is to privilege ordinary experience, showing how political decisions and policies, including geopolitical factors, affect people at the level of the village and street.

Chapter 1 takes the reader to the scene of the devastating earthquake of December 7, 1988. In chapter 2 we travel to Azerbaijan and hear from Armenians who were attacked in January 1988, as well as those who survived subsequent pogroms that forced them to emigrate. In chapter 3 we examine the war in Nagorno-Karabakh and the independence movement that prompted the pogroms against Armenians living in Azerbaijan. Chapter 4 describes the daily life of Armenians living in Yerevan—the bitter cold, the lack of food, the effects of the dismal economy on the people. The book concludes with two chapters that are more analytical in focus—probing the humanistic elements of the preceding chapters, including the moral and spiritual choices that people made in response to their situation—and an epilogue that updates the research to the end of the first decade after the Republic of Armenia declared independence.

The appendixes present our methodology, interview questions, and a list of interviewees, but several elements of the research and writing process should be mentioned here. First, the sample of interviewees was not random; it was a snowball sample that varied by location. For example, we took the research team to Stepanakert, where they spent four days intensively interviewing refugees who filled a large hotel. Later, one member of the team returned to Stepanakert for a month and interviewed a broader range of people, this time residents of the city. In the earthquake zone, we took overnight trips to both Spitak and Gyumri, where we knocked on people's doors and asked if we could interview them; they invariably welcomed team members into their homes. Yerevan had housing settlements with high concentrations of refugees, so we went there to interview Armenians from Azerbaijan. Concerning the winter, the team interviewed friends, professors, and people on the street. Everyone had a story to tell and an opinion to offer.

The typical interview lasted slightly over an hour. The research team had an interview guide to follow, but beyond that the interviews were very open-ended. We simply encouraged people to tell their stories within the broader theme that was the subject of the interview—the war, the earthquake, the blockade, and refugees. Each interview began with a brief explanation of the project and a request to tape-record the interview. Interviewees were then asked if they wished to remain anonymous (only a few did). Finally, everyone signed a release form giving permission for their story to be used in the book and in other scholarly projects.

Moral Issues

Writing this book has been an emotional experience, often reminding us of the process of researching and writing our book on the Armenian genocide. We found it very difficult to distance ourselves from these first-person accounts, especially when parents talked about the plight of their children or when children described the loss of their parents. Death, violence, and suffering may be universal, but we seldom experience them, even vicariously, in such intense doses. The stories told here are painful. But they are also a call to give thanks for the gifts of life, to value the promises of the moment, and to realize one's humanity by helping someone in need.

Throughout the book we ask, usually indirectly, whether the liberation of Armenia and Nagorno-Karabakh—an ongoing struggle—has been worth the pain and suffering. There are the obvious casualties of the war, from those who have lost legs and arms to the many women and children without husbands and fathers. And there are also the casualties of the battered economy, a flood of emigrants who may never return. In its depopulated state, with the departure of many of its scientists and professionals, it is questionable whether Armenia remains economically viable. Was independence, then, a hollow victory? We invite the reader to consider this question in light of the views and experiences of the three hundred people we interviewed.

Although we strongly believe in the right of the Armenian people to assert their independence—from the former Soviet Union and, for the Armenians of Nagorno-Karabakh, from the rule of the Republic of Azerbaijan—we do not intend to promote a political agenda. Our focus is on the human dimension of the conflict and its moral repercussions. We have sympathy for the million or so Azerbaijanis who live in refugee camps because they, too, have been displaced by the war in Nagorno-Karabakh. But at the same time, we must condemn warfare that targets civilian populations, as did the attacks on Nagorno-Karabakh by the Azerbaijani government, which violates one of the fundamental principles of the just war doctrine. And we find no moral justification for a blockade that is suffocating the economy and therefore producing mass emigration from Armenia.

The issues associated with Armenian independence are common to people in almost all of the former Soviet republics, as well as to ethnic groups in other parts of the world. In the midst of death, hunger, cold, and violence, the human spirit emerges in all its profound beauty and complexity. Thus, although it is a case study of a recent independence struggle, this book also explores elements of human experience that are far deeper than political events. The earthquake puts us in touch with our vulnerability to natural disaster; the pogroms in Azerbaijan remind us that civilization rests on a thin veneer of law and order controlling the baser human instincts; the war in Nagorno-Karabakh confronts us with the cost of independence and the pain of violent struggle; and the Turkish and Azerbaijani blockade demonstrates the potential for cruelty of the strong against the weak. This story of the rebirth of a free and independent Armenia addresses the deepest elements of our common humanity—those that bind us to each other regardless of race, ethnicity, or nationality.

Massive Destruction

The 1988 Earthquake

On December 7, 1988, at 11:41 A.M., a devastating earthquake struck northwestern Armenia. Registering 6.9 on the Richter scale, the earthquake lasted forty seconds and was followed four minutes later by a 5.8 magnitude aftershock and swarms of smaller quakes, some as strong as 5.0. Four cities and fifty-eight villages were affected in an area with a diameter of eighty kilometers. At least 25,000 people were killed (this is the Soviet figure), and estimates run as high as 100,000. Many thousands were injured, and at least 500,000 were left homeless. Direct economic loss was estimated at $14.2 billion, and 40 percent of Armenia's industrial capacity was destroyed, affecting the economic livelihood of hundreds of thousands of Armenians. It was the worst earthquake to hit the region since 1046, although other major earthquakes had been recorded in 1899 and 1940 within one hundred kilometers of the epicenter of the 1988 quake.

Spitak was the city hardest hit. More than 5,000 buildings were destroyed, including 30 five-story commercial structures in the center of the town. Many of these buildings flattened like pancakes, killing nearly every

Earthquake debris outside of Spitak.

person inside. In this town of approximately 25,000 people, about 20 percent of the population was killed. In School Number 1, 14 teachers and 53 pupils were killed. In the village of Shirakamut, nothing remained standing, and 112 children and teachers were killed in the middle school. The survival of those who were not killed on impact but were trapped in the rubble was threatened by temperatures that dipped to 20°F at night. Several days passed before international rescue teams with dogs and temperature-sensitive devices arrived. Unfortunately, nearly all of the hospitals were destroyed, and 80 percent of local medical professionals lost their lives in the quake. When rescue equipment finally arrived, the communications infrastructure was virtually nonexistent, fuel was scarce, and the sheer size of the disaster made coordination difficult. A week after the quake, 19,000 people, among them 5,400 survivors, had been extracted from the debris.

The first rescuers to arrive were residents from nearby Yerevan, and shortly thereafter teams arrived from several Soviet republics. For the first time since 1923, the Soviet Union invited the help of international relief organizations, and the relief effort was later referred to as the "fall of the humanitarian wall" in the former Soviet Union. The outpouring

Girl in front of her school in Spitak.

of foreign assistance was remarkable. Almost immediately, France sent
22 doctors and 21 dogs, and Switzerland sent 37 well-equipped rescue
and medical personnel. Red Cross groups from around the world sent
tents, stretchers, medicine, kitchen utensils, and other supplies. By early
January, the United Nations estimated that help had come from 111 countries; 7 international organizations; 53 national chapters of the Red Cross;
3,600 foreign specialists; 1,500 rescuers and firefighters from 15 countries; 230 physicians, surgeons, psychiatrists, and psychologists from 12
countries; and 22 rescue teams from 21 countries. Individuals, organizations, and national governments had pledged $113 million in aid, ex-
cluding in-kind aid such as search-and-rescue teams, and there had been
1,400 relief flights, 335 of them from abroad. By January 2, the number
of people extracted from the ruins had grown to 40,000. Estimates a
month after the quake described Spitak as nearly totally destroyed; the
cultural center of Armenia, Gyumri (then Leninakan), as 80 percent destroyed or damaged; and the industrial town of Vanadzor (then Kiro-
vakan) as 50 percent destroyed or damaged. In Spitak and Gyumri, 105
of the 131 schools were unusable.

Journalists and rescue team workers told heartrending stories. A team from the United States discovered a sixty-year-old woman who was pinned at the knees by heavy concrete and rubble. Sandwiched against her were a dead infant and a young girl. In order to extract the grandmother, rescuers first had to amputate the leg of her deceased granddaughter. This was not an unusual occurrence; cranes and heavy equipment did not arrive in large numbers until December 17, ten days after the quake, and consequently extreme measures had to be taken to free people from the debris.

An Ameri-Cares worker described the soccer field in Spitak. Coffins filled the stadium seats, waiting for someone to claim the victims within. He said that a yellow car arrived bearing four men who silently got out, went to the grandstand lined with thousands of coffins, lifted lid after lid, and finally knelt in front of a small coffin, bowed their heads, and then carried the box to their car. Other observers said that coffins were stacked up on street corners, eventually to be carried away by family members, who tied them to the roofs of their cars. A shortage of caskets meant that some people were buried without one. When whole families had been killed, sometimes no one was left to bury them.

Rescuers often felt helpless. Multistory buildings listed at 10 to 20 degrees, and they were simply too dangerous to enter, especially with the aftershocks that kept coming. Some buildings had completely collapsed, and there was no way to enter them. Many were prefabricated buildings, and the engineering was woefully substandard for earthquake territory. Floors were inadequately connected to vertical beams, so when the earth shook, one floor collapsed on top of another, killing everyone in between.

Spitak

Five years after the earthquake, we took our research team to Spitak, and later to Gyumri, to interview survivors about their experiences. We had been to Spitak previously, two years after the earthquake, and remembered driving several kilometers, passing a cemetery filled with burial stones bearing photographic likenesses of children and loved ones who had died. These stone markers brought home the reality of the tens of thousands of people who had been struck down in the prime of life. We particularly remembered etched images of children carrying school bags, and one of a little girl holding a handful of flowers. Every one of these stone monuments represented a void in the life of someone still living,

Gravestone in Spitak.

and so we wondered what we would encounter in 1993. Had the wounds healed? Were people getting on with their lives? It did not take long for these questions to be answered.

Twelve of us had crowded into the minivan to make the two-hour drive to Spitak from Yerevan. As we dropped off members of our research team at various locations to interview survivors of the earthquake, we looked for a restaurant where the team could have dinner. The options were limited. Much of the downtown area was still in ruins. The first place we approached had no bread, although the owners graciously offered us a glass of bottled soda. We succeeded, however, on our second attempt. The house specialty was *khengali*, a meat pastry baked in broth, and the owner had a wood stove where he could cook if there was no electrical power. While negotiating the price of our meals, we asked if we could hire some local musicians for the evening. Our research team had been working hard for several months, and we thought that this might be a moment to celebrate. We felt embarrassed, however, when Tavit, the owner, told us that in Spitak there had been no live entertainment since the earthquake. Although five years had passed, people were obviously still mourning.

That evening, as the research team gathered for dinner, the electricity was indeed off. We sat by candlelight at a long table filled with locally grown herbs, bread, cheese, Armenian brandy, and, as the meal unfolded, the promised *khengali.* In spite of the somber interviews of the daylight hours, the mood was celebratory. Our son Shont was along on this trip, and it was his twentieth birthday, so he was the recipient of many toasts. In the midst of dinner, suddenly the lights flickered on. Everyone cheered! And, to our surprise, Tavit started playing an Armenian tape on a small stereo. Spontaneously our research team, all graduate students in their middle to late twenties, began to dance. Even Shont was dragged to his feet by one of the women. And then all eyes turned to Tavit. In the corner of the room he was dancing, his tall, lanky frame lithely revealing something we had not known: before the earthquake Tavit had been a dance instructor. As we left the restaurant sometime after midnight, one of the waiters whispered to us that this was the first time he had seen Tavit dance in five years, since his wife had died in the earthquake, leaving him with two small children to raise.

Reconstruction and Rehabilitation

In addition to delivering aid immediately after the earthquake, many countries and organizations made commitments to assist with reconstruction. In Spitak, for example, the Norwegians constructed a hospital. The Russians built 133 homes; the Uzbeks, 124; the Estonians, 80; the Norwegians, 23; and the Swiss and Armenians together, 260. In addition, several countries helped provide long-term rehabilitation for people with limb amputations, paralysis, and spinal cord injuries, including care of survivors who were brought to the United States. Psychological support was provided for people suffering from post-trauma stress, and many outsiders, including diaspora Armenians trained in this area, helped children, in particular, to deal with their anxieties.

A high percentage of children suffered from sleep disturbances, separation anxiety, nightmares, regressive behavior, withdrawal, and general expressions of distrust, pessimism, and hopelessness. Children not only lost parents, relatives, and playmates, but they also witnessed horrific scenes of people trapped under rubble. They were frightened by aftershocks, which sometimes were accompanied by strange underground rumbling sounds. Many children, as well as adults, were afraid to enter multistory structures after the quake. Moreover, normal patterns of

Girl playing in earthquake ruins in Spitak.

everyday life had collapsed. Schools were destroyed, so children were left with little to do. And some observers said that post-trauma stress was exacerbated by the tendency of Armenian culture to emphasize silent heroic suffering and the denial of pain and weakness. Survivors were reluctant to tell children the truth about losses incurred by the extended family.

Unfortunately, most reconstruction ground to a halt after 1990. After the collapse of the Soviet Union, Russian workers went home. Furthermore, the blockade of Armenia by Turkey and Azerbaijan made it nearly impossible to bring building materials into the country. When we visited Gyumri in 1993, a town of about 200,000 people, we saw half-completed construction projects everywhere. Rusted cranes pointed skyward. The clock in the town square was still stopped at exactly 11:41. It was a depressing sight, because obviously there had been substantial goodwill in the aftermath of the earthquake. Yet it seemed that the war in Nagorno-Karabakh and the corresponding blockade had nullified these intentions. For example, ten years after the earthquake, 17,500 people in Gyumri were still living in temporary housing. Industry was working at only 20 to 30 percent of its former capacity. Furthermore, Gyumri was

Boys in homemade car outside of *domigs* near Gyumri.

forced to absorb 30,000 Armenian refugees who had fled the pogroms in Baku and Sumgait. In Nalband, 250 of the 300 homes being constructed were not completed by the Russians. Spitak was more fortunate. Of the 5,100 buildings that were destroyed, 1,400 had been reconstructed. But this still left many people living in primitive housing.

We visited some of the shipping containers and *domigs* (pipelike houses) that people were living in after the quake. Never intended as permanent homes, they were small and cramped, lacked decent insulation, and were subject to leaks. However, individuals were afraid to reconstruct homes out of stone, because without proper steel reinforcement, even one-story houses could not stand up to another quake. We saw the ruins of hundreds of such homes—mere rock piles, often with a few roof timbers sticking up at random angles. Ironically, some of the structures still standing were the oldest buildings, constructed prior to the Soviet era. Corruption played some role in the failure of the modern buildings, as contractors cheated on the amount of cement that went into the concrete as well as on the extent of steel reinforcement. The more fundamental problem, however, was inadequate engineering, with brittle or nearly nonexistent fasteners linking floors to upright beams.

Abandoned construction site in Gyumri.

Domigs serving as temporary housing near Gyumri.

The Day of the Earthquake

The events of December 7, 1988, were etched in the minds of everyone we interviewed. People described what they were doing immediately prior to the quake: making tea, working in a factory, teaching children in school.

Some people first thought they were being shelled by Azerbaijan. A woman from Gyumri said, "Ninety percent of the teachers in the school felt that this was bombing, shelling by the Turks, because the relations between Azeris and Armenians weren't good at all during those days." This perception was compounded by the fact that some of the wives of soldiers serving in the army did not come to school that day, she said, "thinking that there would be a conflict between Azeris and Armenians." Another person said, "All the military with their families left the area. Those who remained stayed in tents rather than in buildings. So it seems like they knew that it was coming." Describing the sound of the earthquake, an individual from Gyumri said, "It was such a powerful noise, we thought it was a bomb explosion, and we felt sure the enemy, the Turks, were on us." However, as soon as they felt the earth rolling and, if they were inside, felt structures continue to shake, most people realized that it was an earthquake.

The typical response was to bolt for a door and try to get outside. In the process, some people fell down because the shaking was so violent. One person thought he was feeling unstable and sick from having drunk too much the night before; others experienced a wave of nausea.

A teacher said that she quickly ushered her students through a doorway, but when she got to the stairs, the stairwell had collapsed, killing some of the children below. She and her students were able to escape through a broken window. A teacher in Gyumri, which was not hit as hard as Spitak, said, "The children ran for me, instead of running out. So I directed them outside, and we all ran out." Then, she said, "They just took off, ran away." Parents, of course, rushed to the schools to try to find their children, but some of the children had run home to find their parents, so there were anxious moments before they were reunited. Some children arrived home to see their houses in ruins, discovering family members who were trapped or dead. Several children from a school in Gyumri who had stayed home sick that day were killed, whereas there were no casualties at the school itself.

An older woman said that she had been visiting a boarding school in Gyumri on the day of the earthquake. She had just finished meeting with the principal when the shaking started. "We realized it was an earthquake. Right away we tried to get all the children out of that building. Thank God the building did not fall down. So we were able to save some three hundred children." They were calming the children outside when the second tremor hit, and a nine-story building across the street came tumbling down. "What a sight!" she said. "I can describe it as though it were hell. People just collapsing under the ruins, and people screaming. Families getting caught under those ruins. It was terrible. . . . You could see death everywhere. People were running and screaming, looking for their loved ones." After the children were sent home, a woman came to the school authorities and said that one of these children went home, only to discover that all of his family had died.

Some people tried to take cover within buildings rather than rush out, but the violent shaking sometimes made this impossible. For example, a woman who was upstairs in her house when the quake hit said that she went underneath a table, but seeing that the walls were falling, she felt that she would be better off if she made a run for it. As soon as she got outside she looked across the street, where a large building had housed a printing press, and saw the building was leveled. She then went to a nearby town where her daughter and daughter-in-law lived. Both of their houses were in ruins. "It took three days before they got my daughter out—her body, that is—and seven days before they got my daughter-in-law out." She had a lingering memory of her daughter's arm sticking out of the rubble. "I recognized her arm. I knew that she was gone, and my son was with me, and he said, 'Mom, let's go home. Let's go home.'"

When asked about her house, she said that she and her relatives were able to salvage some furniture, which was more than many people could do. They were able to get out some food, too. Then, she said, "I went to my daughter-in-law's and salvaged clothing, as much as we could. We did it real fast, because it wasn't safe." At night they stayed outside because of the threat of further quakes. "So we lit a fire, stayed outside in the street. We had the beds, and we had quilts, and we covered ourselves." When asked what her grandchildren remember about the earthquake, she said that one grandson had vivid recollections.

My daughter's son, he was in kindergarten and when the earthquake took place they were told to run out, and they did, to the outside. They got out of the building, but thank God the building didn't fall down. They were safe outside in the yard, and my grandson remembers very well. He waited and waited. Mom had taken him to kindergarten, and mom had to come and pick him up. But there was no mom. Finally a neighbor came and picked him up and took him to my sister's house, and that's where he realized that mom was gone. That mom wasn't going to come. He realized that mom was dead, and he cried and he wanted his mom.

At this point the grandmother broke down. Tears came to her eyes. When our interviewer asked her whether she could find any comfort now, she replied, "Maybe from my kids. I don't know." She also said that she turned to God after the earthquake, saying, "I don't know how. It just so happens that I believe in God now." Not trying to make a rational argument, but just reporting her observations, she said, "Before the quake there weren't that many believers, but after the quake many came to believe in God."

Although aftershocks continued, people immediately set about the task of recovering loved ones, getting them to the hospital or medical care, burying the dead, and salvaging whatever they could from the ruins. A mother said that her son was trapped on the fifth floor of a nine-story apartment building, and she could hear him shouting for help. Her husband and their thirteen-year-old son dug with their bare hands until they got to the child and rescued him, but, unfortunately, the husband fell two stories to his death while escaping the damaged building. Another woman described how her husband was buried under books and collapsed walls in a hallway. Rescuers decided that it would be best to tunnel underground to reach him, and so friends rallied together, dug a tunnel, and got him out. Another survivor recalled individuals frantically working into the night. "I remember people were saving a four-year-old boy with the headlights of a truck at night, and my son and I saw it, and he came out alive from under the ruins." Describing the rescue efforts, one person said, "It was primitive. All done by hands and by home tools. [There was] nothing big, no huge machinery to save the injured."

When heavy machinery did arrive, the tractors and cranes made so much noise that they were often shut down so that people could listen for signs of life and calls for help. Unfortunately, many injured individuals did not survive the rescue attempt.

> My oldest daughter was in her own house with her two-and-a-half-year-old child. They were both killed. My sons were able to go and unearth them. It was awful to see them dead. My daughter's eyes were kind of . . . they had an expression of shock. Her chest was smashed, but the rest of her body was okay. My grandchild was killed. It was awful to unearth them and see them in that condition. It was heartbreaking. We had to see them in that condition, and we had to bury them.

Sometimes people took the initiative to save themselves rather than wait for help. A particularly poignant example is of a woman who used shattered glass within reach to cut off her own arm in order to free herself. In contrast, a woman left hanging upside down by her legs ended up losing her life because people hesitated to cut off her legs in order to liberate her, even though she begged them to. The reluctance to amputate limbs with crude implements may have led to other deaths as well. As one person said, "I remember a man was caught under the rubble, and part of his body was out and part was under, and they tried so hard to get him, even thinking of cutting limbs to save him, but this didn't work and he died."

Injured and trapped people were sometimes ignored, simply because everyone was caught up in their own attempts to survive or rescue family members. One woman confessed, "I remember just running by dead people, not paying any attention, jumping over them just so I could go and find my sons." Rescuers from nearby Yerevan sometimes could not be very helpful because, not having realized the magnitude of the disaster, they had failed to bring equipment to extricate people from rubble and were not prepared to stay through the cold nights. Furthermore, many interviewees reported that people were in a dazed state, suffering from shock, and could not work efficiently in the early hours of the rescue operation. In fact, quite a few people said that rescue attempts seemed chaotic and disorganized. One person complained that there was sometimes a language barrier. "English people came and people from Poland and Ukraine. They worked very hard. The sad thing was that there was no one to translate what they were saying. So they had to work with their dogs. Their dogs would be the ones to identify if there were people alive under the ruins."

Medical personnel had no option but to triage the injured. A woman who had broken bones in her arms but was in stable condition said, "You see, they were taking care of the worst victims. They were paying more attention to the worst hurt, taking them first, and so on down the line." Only a little time could be given to each patient; consequently, this woman ended up with casts that resulted in crooked arms that still hurt. In retrospect, however, she forgave the doctors because of the stress they were under. "In the hospital, when I was there, constantly victims were being brought. With legs missing, arms broken. It was just awful. Victim after victim. There were lots of doctors, both Armenian and Russian, helping the victims." As soon as possible, the injured were taken to Yerevan and then to Moscow; some were taken to specialty hospitals in Europe and the United States.

At the same time, as is true in any calamity, opportunists exploited the situation. More than one person mentioned looting that occurred and the theft of people's valuables, including jewelry, from the rubble of their homes. The most flagrant example of preying on misfortune was offered by a citizen of Gyumri. With the aid of a Russian soldier, a man had unearthed his wife from the ruins. The Russian soldier saw another man come and fall on her, crying, "My dear wife," and so on, while simultaneously trying to loosen her jewelry. "The Russian realized that this guy was stealing, and he realized that it wasn't the right husband and killed him on the spot. . . . This guy looting a dead woman and pretending she is his wife. It was awful." This same person reported equally disturbing events: "Other cases happened where people buried women who had jewelry before their loved ones arrived to identify them. When the loved ones came, they couldn't find them; they had already been buried. But the people who had buried them did that so they could steal their jewelry and it wouldn't be found out."

Such reactions were deviant, however. More prevalent in our interviews was the emphasis on people's grief, felt at the time of the earthquake and afterward. A mother reportedly died on the spot, perhaps from heart failure, when rescuers excavating a location found one of her children alive and the other one dead. Reactions to the trauma were often delayed, however, as indicated by one woman's reflections on her father's death.

> He was not injured, but emotionally, spiritually, he was so affected by the earthquake that it took its toll on him, and he died because he was an eyewitness to the deaths of many students where he worked. The school was destroyed, and many children lost their lives. This was too much for my father, even though none of us, brothers or sisters or my mother, were killed. But he saw too much tragedy, too much death where he worked, and it just killed him very shortly after the earthquake.

And then there were people who did not die but wished they had. A woman from Gyumri said, "One time I met this blind lady, and she was crying, actually wailing. I felt so sorry for her. I asked her, 'What's wrong?' and she said that her husband and her son and her daughter-in-law were all killed in the earthquake, and she was left all alone. She was wailing, and she was singing as she was crying. It was strange." This person said, "I talked to her several times. I asked again and again, 'How can I help you?' And she said, 'All I need, all I want, is death. I don't want to live. God left me here to grieve.' It was pathetic." This same person said she talked to another woman immediately after the earthquake. "She said she had lost all her family, and she was the sole survivor. She had lost her children, grandchildren. It was awful. And her wealth, as well. She said, now she had nothing, just her body, just herself."

And, of course, there were the losses experienced by children. A grandmother described an orphan girl who ran up to her one day and said, "You know what? I saw my mom! I saw my mom!" This woman said she felt so sorry for this little girl because she then said, "I saw my mom. She was driving by, but she did not look at me." Such fantasies were the direct result of uncompensated emotional loss.

One Person's Account

Abstracting elements from interviewees' stories is useful, but it fails to describe the day-by-day struggle to live and find meaning that marked the experience of survivors. The following account of a woman from Gyumri portrays the pattern of life before the earthquake in contrast to what it was like afterward.

> You see, Armenouhy was home with me, and I was ironing. Then we had to go shopping, so she came with me. We went shopping, and I got a few things, and I said, "Armenouhy, why don't you go home, and I'll get the rest, and then I'll come back?" She kept saying no. Finally I convinced her, and she went home. While I was doing the rest of the shopping, I realized that I had the key and had forgotten to give it to her. I thought, "Oh no! What's going to happen?" Anyway, while I was still in the store, the earthquake hit. The shaking was so powerful, the ground under our feet was moving back and forth, and all of us were just confused. I did not know what was happening. I thought it was my head. I was getting dizzy.
>
> Then I ran out of the store, and the first thing I could think of was my son Hovannes in school. So I wildly ran to find out where he was. His school was not so far. So I ran to the school, and I saw the teacher, and the teacher said, "You know, Hovannes is okay. I sent him home."
>
> So I started going toward our home, and sure enough, I found my son. We hugged. I was so happy to see him alive. He said, "Mom, sister Vartouhy's house is all destroyed. It is in ruins." We ran there, and sure enough, the five-story house was all in ruins. My daughter was crushed under the rubble. She was pregnant, expecting her first child. I knew she was gone in a matter of minutes. My brother came and helped move the ruins, the rocks, and we found my daughter dead. Then I ran to our home, and that was gone. All five floors were ruined. Now my concern was Armenouhy. I looked for Armenouhy. I did not find her.

Armenouhy was under the rubble of their house. For the next five days, while people tried to remove the stones, this mother said that she just sat there and cried, saying, "She is alive. She is alive. Please get her out of the ruins." In the meantime, a Swedish rescue team came with their dogs and a heat-sensing device and determined that her daughter was, indeed, still alive.

> "Yes," they said. "There is life in here." They had machines, and they were able to cut it open. Sure enough, I saw the curly hair of my daughter, and she was alive. I was so happy, but they would not let us touch her. They were able to get one arm out. The other arm they could not. They gave her intravenous feeding. They gave her water. I watched that. There was one broken leg. It took them three to four hours to free her from the ruins. When they brought her out from the ruins, they closed her eyes, and they would not let us touch her. They said, "She has to go to the hospital."

Armenouhy was taken to Yerevan, and after two months in a hospital, she was sent to the United States for treatment. The other daughter was buried immediately and without a casket, because wood was scarce due to the number of people who had died. "It was awful to see her buried without a casket. To this day I cry, because I know that she did not get a good burial. Time and again I have asked that we take her body and give her a decent burial by her in-laws. It is awful, just awful, to lose your child in the earthquake." Later in the interview she summed up the effects of the earthquake on their family situation: "We lost our salary, we lost our home, we lost our lives, and now we are left with one handicapped child."

Her husband was hospitalized because of his "nerves," and Armenouhy lives a difficult life. Her mother said, "Yes, they had to amputate one leg, and she cannot hear well. She is a very nervous girl. She used to be very athletic and very active, but now she is very frustrated and often very nervous." In part, her nervousness is obviously a product of the social situation in which she now lives. Her mother recalled the change that occurred after she returned from the United States.

> I remember in Yerevan, when she was in the hospital, she would just stare at us and not talk. Her gaze was very severe and unusual, and she was one of the most severely injured cases. So they took her on the plane. She was practically paralyzed, and she stayed five months in the United States. She really revived. When she came back, she was on her feet. We were so surprised to see her on her feet. So well dressed. She brought flowers for me, and she really had a good time there. Any time that she is bored or does not know what to do, she gets all her pictures out that she took in the United States. She will say, "This is my friend and this is my friend." These

are the people she enjoyed. She made friends over there. She was well taken care of, well treated medically, and it was a very good experience for her there.

When our interviewer tried to console this mother by suggesting that perhaps Armenouhy might eventually get married, and her life would turn around, the response was pragmatic: "She can't get married, because how can she take care of her baby if she is missing a leg and an arm and cannot hear?" With a spirit of both determination and resignation, she then said, "I take care of her now, and I will take care of her until I die." But she also wondered, understandably, who would take care of her daughter after she died, saying, "I wish she would die the same time I die."

Aid from Abroad

The immediate emotional shock from losing loved ones is traumatic, but whereas after most personal calamities there is a job to return to and a stable network of institutions and friends, an earthquake of this magnitude disrupts all aspects of daily life. In addition to losing children, spouses, relatives, and friends, many people lost the contents of their homes. They did not even have utensils to eat with, let alone clothing or personal effects. We heard some comments on the general appearance of people in the aftermath of the earthquake: men were unshaven, and most people walked around in dirty and often tattered clothing. Furthermore, jobs evaporated, all forms of entertainment instantly disappeared, and churches were destroyed. In short, living patterns were shattered, and with them the meaning and personal satisfaction they imparted. After a crisis of this magnitude, physical intervention is important for immediate survival, but reconstruction of social structures—community, employment, education— is equally important.

As already noted, aid came from all over the world. Those we interviewed were grateful for this assistance, but they also offered qualifications. For one thing, many people questioned whether the gifts actually reached victims, or whether various intermediaries, including the government, siphoned off aid for their personal benefit. This statement is typical: "It is unfortunate, but it is true. A lot of clothing came from overseas, and those who didn't need it snatched it away. It was sad. Yes, it did not get to its destination in many cases. Man is greedy, and it was

Church in Gyumri.

obvious even then." People also mentioned that aid may have been delivered to other victims, but they themselves did not receive it. For example, a teacher said, "I heard that a lot of pens and pencils were sent. Loads of them. But I'm a teacher, and I had a lot of students, and we never got any. I feel very strongly that our officials took what was sent. They used it for their own profit."

On the other hand, a lot of aid obviously did reach victims of the earthquake. Several people mentioned that they refused it because they felt the needs of other people were more severe.

> I applied to the church, myself. That's the only place I applied for help. But when I returned [to get the aid], I felt so bad. I thought, "No, I don't need their help. Let them help other people in worse conditions. I am going to work hard and support my children." I would rather do it with my own hard work, rather than ask for alms.

There was also a sentiment among survivors of the earthquake that, while they needed immediate assistance, direct aid was a short-term solution. One man said, quite specifically, "I don't want handouts. We need aid in the form of work, where we can work and provide for our fami-

Consequences of the earthquake and economic collapse in Spitak—nothing to do and nowhere to go.

lies." He said that it makes one lazy to simply sit and wait for assistance from outsiders. Another person echoed this same conviction: "I am not for that kind of help, where they come and just respond to a need. I'd rather see them come and do something. Get involved, get the people involved in some kind of work, some kind of skill, some kind of production." He went on to say, "What we need, the best help that we would profit from, is technical help. I wish these foreign countries would bring technical help. Then that would profit everybody."

A significant amount of assistance came from relatives who were living outside of the earthquake zone. Scores of people drove to the hard-struck cities and villages within hours of hearing the news. They came to check on relatives and to provide whatever assistance they could, which was sometimes minimal, since they often did not have appropriate tools with them. A man from Yerevan said, "Yes, I did go to help with the rescue efforts. All we had were our hands, and we had to dig and rescue the victims. I remember awful scenes. At times we would reach victims, and other times we couldn't. There would be cries, but by the time we'd get to them, they would already be dead." In fact, many of the rescuers that we interviewed seemed as traumatized by what they had observed as the people who were directly affected by the quake. They returned home almost shell-shocked. The devastation that had occurred, the deaths they had observed in their rescue attempts, and the calamity that had struck families was beyond belief.

A woman said that the traffic was so bad along the route to the earthquake area that she waited a few days before going. But the scenes she encountered once there left her shaken. "People were glad just to find body parts of their loved ones. In other words, if they found an arm or leg or part of the body, they were glad, saying, 'At least I have found part of my beloved one.' Can you imagine just how terrible that was?" She said that these scenes affected her. "I had such awful, strong headaches. My blood pressure shot straight up, and I couldn't return right away. It affected me something terrible. I remember that for a whole month I wasn't myself. I was just sick, grieving with these people." She kept struggling with two scenes in particular: "There was this fifty-year-old lady crying. She was crying, saying, 'At least let me find one part of my child so I can bury him.'" She also remembered seeing "this kid taking water and bread to the cemetery, thinking that his loved one would eat it and think it. The cemetery was just full. You couldn't even drop a needle in it."

One woman's brother had gone to help quake victims, and when he returned he could not even speak about what he had seen. "He came back totally in shock. We asked him to tell us what had happened or what he had seen, but he couldn't talk. He couldn't sleep. He was just so upset about the whole thing." Another woman said that what she saw in Gyumri would stay with her the rest of her life. "It looked as if the whole town had been mixed with a huge spoon." Riding in a car with a survivor, she said that the two of them were hugging each other and shaking. "There were coffins everywhere. Many, many coffins. Near the destroyed houses the rescue workers were continuing—they were searching for people." She remembered especially one man who was down on his knees in front of the ruins of his house, crying loudly for his loved ones under the rubble. Another man, an engineer, went to Gyumri from Yerevan to see about his relatives. He unearthed twenty-four members of his family—grandchildren, cousins, and so on—and when he returned home he became ill and was virtually speechless, unable to express what he had experienced.

A woman said that her husband, too, was unable to talk when he returned from Gyumri. It was only later that the stories started to spill out. For example, her husband and others tried to free a man whose foot was caught under a rock in the ruins of a building. A military doctor insisted that they simply cut off the foot. However, her husband argued that they could save him another way, and, in fact, they did. This same woman said that another friend hanged himself after returning from Gyumri. He had tried to rescue children from a school that had collapsed and simply could not bear the grief of that experience.

Another man from Yerevan described feeling paralyzed on the day he arrived in Spitak. "We couldn't do anything on our first day there because we were in shock. The city was literally covered with corpses. I cannot describe the horror we felt. There are no words to describe it." He said that his worst experience was searching for the bodies of children in a kindergarten. He also recalled a young boy who ran to him and wanted him to help unearth the body of his mother, who was dead. Indeed, all of the rescuers that we interviewed had memories they could not shake off.

One of the most touching recollections was that of a young father who had gone to Spitak from Yerevan to help with the rescue effort. He said that he got somewhat lost walking back to sleep for the night, in part because familiar landmarks were no longer there.

> It was quite dark, and in the dark I saw a little candlelight. I approached to see what was going on. I saw this boy beside a stick with a picture of a dead person. It must have been his father. He was just sitting by it with a candle, with his head in his hands. Boy, did that sight ever grieve me. I cannot forget that poor boy. Just sitting at a vigil with the dead in the candlelight, holding his head in his hands. What a sight. What a tragedy.

This same man said that he removed debris from collapsed buildings, but when they discovered corpses, he simply was not able to touch them. Others had to do it. He also told of uncovering a man who was not injured, and immediately this man started working with the team to unearth more people. He evidently had family members or fellow workers who were still under the rubble.

The Political Context

The earthquake should not be understood as an isolated event. It occurred during Armenia's struggle for independence and Nagorno-Karabakh's quest for liberation. Before the earthquake, Armenian refugees from Azerbaijan had settled in Spitak, Gyumri, and Vanadzor, and in adjacent areas. After the earthquake, the conflict in Nagorno-Karabakh and the Turkish and Azerbaijani blockade—along with dramatic changes transpiring in the Soviet Union—brought reconstruction to a halt by 1991, leaving thousands of people to live in temporary shelters that were completely inadequate for Armenia's cold winters and hot summers. Even more difficult were the subsequent winters without adequate fuel or food. If one had tried to invent a more disastrous confluence of events, it would have been difficult. One of the worst natural disasters of contemporary history was followed by the blockade of a landlocked country—a country, moreover, that was experimenting with new democratic institutions as it struggled to convert from Soviet communism to free market capitalism.

Furthermore, we cannot ignore the role politics played in the aftermath of this earthquake. Soviet isolation had kept engineers from following contemporary standards of earthquake construction. A similar quake in Los Angeles would cause few, if any, deaths, because older buildings have been retrofitted and new ones designed to withstand large earthquakes. Furthermore, Armenia had no emergency plan. The Karabakh Committee, which was leading the independence movement, assumed leadership of disaster relief before Gorbachev arrived in Yerevan on December 10. Gorbachev proceeded to have members of the Karabakh Committee locked up for the next six months in a Moscow jail, eventually releasing them without a trial. It is also tragic that the Soviet army scarcely lent a hand in the rescue operations, sometimes neglecting even to shine the lights of their vehicles on excavation work at night. We heard reports of the Soviet military turning back the cars of people coming to help, even smashing in their headlights with the butts of their rifles.

One must remember the political events of 1988. Mass demonstrations had filled the streets of Yerevan since February. In fact, on November 7, a month before the earthquake, hundreds of thousands of Armenians had filled Lenin Square in Yerevan to boo at the Communist Party officials who were celebrating the 1917 Revolution; the people launched a counterdemonstration for Armenian independence and union with Nagorno-Karabakh. A state of emergency was declared on November 24, imposing a curfew from 8 P.M. to 6 A.M. From a political standpoint, perhaps it is not surprising that the Soviet military was rather passive in its response to the earthquake.

However, it is a sad commentary on human nature that politics gets in the way of humanitarian responses. Obviously, the biblical story of the Good Samaritan seems to be more often taken to heart by individuals than by national leaders. Nevertheless, the outpouring of support from around the world—although notably not from Armenia's closest neighbors, Turkey and Azerbaijan—was incredible, motivated, in part, by awareness of the failure of the worldwide community to prevent the slaughter of over a million Armenians in 1915.

Ten Years Later

On the occasion of the ten-year commemoration of the earthquake, Spitak was bustling with activity. A new city hall had been constructed. A monument to those who lost their lives in the earthquake had just been completed. Private businesses were building offices that provided a welcome contrast to monotonous Soviet-style architecture. Forty-five percent of the children were in new schools. Most important, the new construction was engineered to withstand an earthquake of 9.0 on the Richter scale, and contractors had carefully followed the specifications. President Robert Kocharian was paying renewed attention to the earthquake, and an ambitious plan had been established for reconstruction of the region. Spitak was something of a showcase, however, and inhabitants of Vanadzor and other areas grumbled about not receiving their fair share of reconstruction funds.

Nevertheless, Spitak still had a long way to go in 1998. Although 1,250 new apartments had been built since the earthquake, only 20 percent of the population was in permanent housing. Many people still lived in shipping containers. However, we saw obvious symbols of international commitment to the area: a Czech-built school, an Italian neighborhood, an Austrian hospital, and a Swiss suburb on the outskirts of town. One news article even indicated that there would be dancing, drinking, and celebration in the town square, which had not occurred since the disaster a decade earlier. In addition to government commitment to rebuilding, philanthropists, such as Kirk Kerkorian, were making substantial funds available for specific projects, as were churches and sister cities outside of Armenia.

Emotional scars left by the earthquake were also healing. Even though employment was still a problem, the social fabric of society was being rewoven. Children were back in school, people were getting married—including men and women who had lost spouses during the quake—and they were once again entertaining neighbors and extended family. There was even a new stone church under construction, replacing the temporary one of sheet metal that had been built to provide a sacred space after the earthquake. People clearly planned to stay here for a while. This was home. They were building for the future.

2

Random Violence

Pogroms in Azerbaijan

Between 1988 and 1990, approximately 350,000 of the 400,000 Armenians living in Azerbaijan emigrated, including some 200,000 refugees who went to the Republic of Armenia. They left Azerbaijan, where many had lived for several generations, because of riots and pogroms against Armenians in both Sumgait and the capital city, Baku. Ironically, Armenians living in Azerbaijan were so thoroughly assimilated that many of them spoke Russian and Azerbaijan as their first and second languages. They would never have abandoned their homes, jobs, and social and cultural relationships had they not felt seriously threatened. But threatened they were—first in Sumgait, in February of 1988, where Armenians were brutally attacked and randomly killed and maimed, and then in Baku, where Armenians were systematically intimidated and made to fear a reprise of Turkish violence against the minority Christian Armenian population.

Genocides and massacres never occur in a political vacuum, and certainly the Sumgait and Baku pogroms were no exception. After Gorbachev announced the complementary principles of glasnost and perestroika, Armenians interpreted the new openness as an invitation to

37

explore the possibility of uniting Nagorno-Karabakh and the Armenian Soviet Socialist Republic (SSR). A petition drive was organized by an informal group that called itself the Karabakh Committee, and on September 18, 1987, half a million people demonstrated in Yerevan, the capital city of Armenia. Five months later, on February 13, 1988, large crowds took to the streets in Stepanakert, the capital city of Nagorno-Karabakh. Within a week, half a million people again gathered in Yerevan, in Theatre Square, to support the call for unification. On February 22, 1988, a counterdemonstration group of Azerbaijanis from the border town Agdam headed toward Stepanakert. According to one version of the story, this group of protestors wreaked havoc on Armenians and their property along the way. But they met resistance, and Armenians killed two Azerbaijanis in the village of Askeran. As the crowd from Agdam fled to their homes, rumors of Armenian brutality circulated, and several days later, on February 27, the Sumgait massacres erupted.

Relations Prior to the Pogroms

Before the Sumgait pogroms, Armenians had lived amicably among Azerbaijanis for more than half a century, in spite of the Turkish massacres of 1918. Typical of the comments we heard was this statement: "We had lots of friends among Azeris, among Armenians. Everything was okay. And overnight, things turned sour and the nightmare began." If anything, before 1988 Azerbaijanis respected Armenians for their industriousness.

> Azeris were okay, they were okay people. We worked together. There were no problems between us up to the month of February, before the uprising. We used to say that they were backward, and we used to tell them, "Why don't you shape up?" As a matter of fact, they used to learn from us. For many things, like clothing and other things, we were their examples. We did it first, and they kind of followed our examples, imitated us. They were backward people, but we did not have problems. I can even say that they were jealous of us, because we were more advanced. They admitted that we were very good in crafts and other things, manufacturing, and in creativity.

Armenians said they were friendly with their neighbors. They often attended Azeri weddings, and it was not unusual for Armenians and Azerbaijanis to intermarry. An Armenian from Baku said, "I had been invited to Azeri weddings, birthday parties, and other celebrations." In his view, "On the surface, everything seemed normal." One Armenian said that before the events of 1988, they scarcely thought about the eth-

Refugee couple living in Yerevan.

nicity of their Azeri neighbors. They related to them as friends, as individuals with personal strengths and weaknesses; there was no particular prejudice against them. Therefore, Armenians were shocked when suddenly they became targets of Azerbaijani aggression because of Armenian cries for independence in Nagorno-Karabakh and then in Yerevan. The attacks did not make sense to them because their relations with Azeri neighbors had not changed. In fact, Azeri friends were often horrified by the events, and they warned Armenians of what they described as "hooligan" activity. Even when Armenians were forced to leave, Azeris sometimes looked after their houses for them or tried to preserve some

Refugee woman near Spitak.

of their possessions. Blanket statements of racist intentions against Armenians by the Azeri population at large are therefore inappropriate. Instead, we must look more carefully at political circumstances and consider the atmosphere created by Gorbachev and the twin policies of perestroika and glasnost, as well as the Azeri government's attitude toward events in Nagorno-Karabakh.

One resident of Sumgait told us that he was aware of meetings held on February 27 during which plans were hatched to attack Armenians. He said, "The main idea was to scare Armenians so that they would not think of or try to work on their independence in Nagorno-Karabakh. They were against our desire to have our own independence." However, he said that Armenians living in Sumgait had no idea that they, personally, would be targeted for violence. "We did not believe, we didn't expect them to get up and kill us. Even though we had heard rumors, we thought, 'No, this cannot happen.' We were not afraid." To explain why he thought they would not be vulnerable as long-time residents in Azerbaijan, he said,

> Why in the world would they do this to us? We were not guilty. We have done nothing in Sumgait. They said they were angry with the Karabakh people and did not want the Karabakh people to become independent.

And here they are, attacking us in Sumgait. We have nothing to do with Karabakh. Why don't they go and fight with the Karabakh people? Here, they are killing us, and we are totally defenseless in our homes.

Throughout the region, populations intermingled; both Armenians and Azeris lived outside the boundaries of their politically identified republics. The Nagorno-Karabakh conflict, however, instigated a drive toward greater homogeneity, and Azeris were pressured to leave Armenia. Some speculate that the displaced Azeris provoked anti-Armenian sentiment, which in turn led to the pogroms. A simpler explanation for the violence in Sumgait and Baku is that Armenians living in Azerbaijan were targets easily labeled "internal enemies," paralleling the response of Americans to their Japanese population during World War II, when citizens of Japanese descent were placed in internment camps.

Sumgait

A Sumgait survivor told our interviewer that she first became alarmed on February 27, when she saw a crowd of teenagers and young adults running around shouting, "Death to the Armenians!" She also saw some of them marking Armenian homes with crosses, working from an address list. By February 28, the massacres were in full swing.

Another resident of Sumgait said that she observed a large crowd of three or four hundred Azerbaijanis enter her village. Following them was a group of armed soldiers from the militia. Her mother returned to their fourth-story apartment from church and reported that an Armenian water vendor had been killed; her husband told her that while he was out buying bread, he saw a store owner beaten and the shop looted. She then heard shots being fired in the distance. At about 4:30 P.M., she went downstairs to telephone the police, because by this time she and her family had heard shouts on the streets and feared an eruption of violence in their neighborhood. However, when she called military headquarters, they assured her that everything was all right, in spite of her insistence that they send someone to investigate. As the noise and sounds of celebration in the streets continued, she again went to call the police, and they told her that the Russian army was coming to quell the violence.

As she headed back upstairs, she met several men carrying her husband down the steps. He was dripping with blood. She rushed past him, looking for her children, and discovered that her apartment was occupied by Azerbaijanis.

> They had taken things [from the house, but] all I was interested in at that time were my children. And I looked at the other bedroom, and the door was shut, and I went and knocked and knocked, and I said, "Children, open up." There was no noise, no sound, and I thought, "What's happening?" I shouted to my children and I called their names. I said, "Roseanne, please open the door. It's mother." And finally they opened it, and I found my three children just scared in their room, and I was happy to see them, and they were happy to see me.

She dressed her children and headed downstairs. On the way down she was struck in the face by a bystander. When she reached the street, she recognized a military friend, who took her and the children to a military station, where they were given tea.

By March 2, Sumgait was quiet, and Armenians were told to gather for bus transport out of the city. The woman who gave the account estimates that some 16,000 to 17,000 people assembled for the journey. Before leaving, however, she ventured back to her apartment to salvage a few belongings, but in her words, "They had taken everything away. All I did was close the door."

Her husband died as a result of his injuries, but her father, who was also beaten severely, survived. She, her mother, and her children were taken to a sanatorium on the Caspian Sea. They stayed there for the month of March, protected by soldiers. Then they were transported to Baku, where they were put in new housing. "They were saying, 'Pick any place in this building that you want to stay and you can live here.' I think they were regretting the slaughter that had taken place in Sumgait. So they were kind to us." Since the family had relatives in Baku, they decided to stay with an aunt. But her father was adamant that they leave Azerbaijan. "He said, 'I am not going to stay in Azerbaijan anymore. I will not be with the Turks anymore. I don't feel safe. They've hurt us enough. Let's get away from here. Let's go to Armenia, to our mother country.' So because of his insistence we all decided to move to Armenia. That's when we came to Armenia, in 1988."

Another survivor of the Sumgait massacres offered a similar account of the events of February 28, 1988:

> Our building was surrounded, and they started breaking our windows and doors. I told my son, "Run for your life. Run for your life, my dear son." And he took off. They had cut our electricity, but not that of the Turks. The killings had begun. . . . I hid in my neighbor's house, and I

Photo carried to Yerevan preserves memories from life in Azerbaijan.

gave away all my jewelry. Had I not, they would have killed me, too. But the soldiers came. As soon as they came, my neighbor, my Turkish neighbor who was hiding me, said, "You've got to go, because the soldiers are here." I found out that the soldiers were carrying the injured, the sick, the hurt to the hospital. I came out and I saw bodies everywhere. They had poured gasoline on them and burned them.

She went to the hospital, and when she returned there was nothing left of her apartment. "Windows were all broken, the doors were broken, the house was destroyed, and they had killed my husband." Later she discovered that her son had also been killed and his body burned.

At this point in her account, she began to weep, but she went on to describe the perpetrators of the violence. She said they were from sixteen to thirty years old and appeared to be drunk, a description that matched the ones offered by other survivors. In assessing the toll on human life, she said that from the ten Armenian families living in their building, eight people were killed. Another survivor cited a similar number. "In our block there were three big apartments: 4, 5, and 6. From those three apartments, twelve people were killed. I can name them one by one."

Grandparents and child in Yerevan. Refugees from Azerbaijan.

We interviewed an Armenian from Baku who went to Sumgait shortly after the massacre to help evacuate his friends, and he reported the following sight: "When we arrived, what had happened was impossible to believe. There were dead bodies on the floor; some were burned alive, some had their chests pierced with a crowbar, some had their ears or heads cut off. It was something unexplainable." When our interviewer asked the man whether he had actually seen these things or had just heard of them, he insisted, "All that I just told you I saw with my own eyes." Other accounts of brutality verified this testimony. Another of our interviewees described a sixty-year-old woman: "They pierced her anus with metal, raped her, and then killed her." This survivor also knew of a girl who had been gang-raped in front of her parents. Still another interviewee cited an acquaintance, six or seven months pregnant, who was raped and then killed.

The following incident is particularly sadistic:

I went to work then, and when I was coming back from work, I saw a pregnant woman in the forty-fifth region. She was naked, and they were raping her and burning her with cigarette butts. When I saw that, I got scared and ran home. My daughter is in a similar condition [i.e., pregnant], and I told her to come to our home, because it is safer and our neighbors would support us.

Our interviewer confirmed that the woman herself had witnessed this. She went on to describe the crowd and their reactions, and added that the woman was finally burned to death.

A student told of a Turkish professor who was very disturbed at having witnessed a similar incident (or possibly the same scene).

> One morning he [the professor] came, and there were one hundred of us in the class, and he said, "How many Armenians do I have in this class?" and six of us stood up, six women, and he acknowledged us, and he said, "A beautiful Armenian like one of you was burned in Sumgait in front of the building. I can still hear her shouts of agony." He cried and said, "I don't understand why Armenians are being killed." He took his books and his notes and he just put them on the desk, and he said, "You know, I cannot lecture today because I am too upset about what is going on in Sumgait." So he just let us go that hour.

Some Armenians attempted to defend themselves. For example, a man who saw an Armenian being thrown from his fourth-floor apartment into a fire burning in the street below said that he realized "they meant business, they were out to kill us." He strung electrical wires on his fence so that if anyone tried to enter his property, they would be electrocuted. Here is his description of what occurred:

> We defended ourselves from 2 P.M. all the way to midnight. These guys were throwing rocks at our apartments. They had rocks piled up outside to destroy our homes, to destroy us. We were in a real battle. The fighting kept on going. They put up a ladder, they got on top of the building, and they turned on the water. They were trying to flood us. I was able to throw the ladder down and fight with them. I was able to stop the water so that we wouldn't be inundated. Some got injured. There were four of us fighting with a whole bunch of them. I was using whatever I could. They hit me with a bottle, and I hit them back with a knife, with jacks that I had. I even injured someone.

During the confrontation he was knifed in the back, but the wound was relatively superficial. His son-in-law, however, was wounded more severely and died the next morning.

> Yes, it was a great loss to us. I wish I had died and he had lived. But I am thankful that I am alive to take care of the children now. Of course, this was a tragedy. Of course, the kids felt it. They saw their dad injured. They saw the body being taken out of the house. That's the reason why one of my grandchildren stammers.

Two Armenian women, in another incident, decided to fight back when their apartment was invaded. Their account reveals that Azerbaijani women were among the attackers (or at least occupiers) of Armenian residences.

> Then I looked on the balcony and there were two Turks. Boy! At this point I was so mad I beat them up; in fact, my mom was there, and she helped me. We beat them up. We threw one over the balcony. I don't know what happened, whether she died or made it. I don't care at this point. And the other Turk just took off. They had no right to be on our balcony, and so that's what I did.

A woman whose husband was killed expressed regret that they had not resisted the attacks. She said,

> The sad thing is that there were so many of us Armenians, and if we had been told ahead of time, we would have all united and fought back. Here we were in Sumgait, totally unprepared. We didn't know what was going on, and we were just killed; my husband was totally unprotected, unprepared, and he was killed. He didn't know what was going on, and he was killed in our house. Had he known, he would have gone and joined the army and fought [presumably in Nagorno-Karabakh], instead of being killed defenselessly. It bothers me to this day that he was killed like that, without knowing, and it was a sudden, cruel killing. If he had known, if we had known, we would have somehow gotten involved, prepared ourselves and resisted, instead of being killed like lambs. What a waste!

Some Armenians defended themselves by trying to pass as Azeris. "My son was approached by them and asked if he was a Turk, and he said that he was and he made up an Azeri name for himself so that they would not kill him. He then managed to escape from the back door and catch a taxi that brought him home." Others said that when they saw the crowd approaching their neighborhood, they got in their car and drove to Baku. Their escape was facilitated by an Azeri friend who volunteered to go with them.

Other Armenians also owed their lives to Azeris who tried to protect them. One woman said, "We had a very kind Turk neighbor. He took us in and hid us. On March 29, it got even worse. They came very close to our building. They were killing Armenians. Our neighbor went out and said that there were no Armenians in this building, where we were hiding." Finally, on April 1, according to this woman, Russian soldiers went door-to-door and collected thousands of Armenians who had been hiding in the homes of friendly and heroic Azerbaijanis.

More than one survivor said that the violence stopped because Russian troops arrived to quell the massacres. Survivors stated repeatedly that the death rate would have been much higher if Azerbaijani neighbors had not protected them. One person we interviewed provided this example: "There was one kind Azerbaijani. This particular man, I saw with my own eyes, he had 25 to 30 Armenian employees and he saved every one of them. He gave them bread and drinks, and he hid them and drove them to safety in his own car." Many Armenians were hidden by neighbors during the peak hours of the massacres and then were helped to escape. One survivor said, "If it wasn't for those kind Turks who hid many Armenians, I don't think that many Armenians would have been left alive. That's what I believe."

Based on the sample of refugees that we interviewed, it appears that Armenians and Azerbaijanis had peacefully coexisted for a number of years. Indeed, they felt secure enough that when the rallies for independence occurred in both Nagorno-Karabakh and Armenia, according to one survivor, "young [Armenian] men with bands on their heads would walk around on the streets shouting: 'Karabakh is ours, Karabakh is ours, Karabakh is ours! It's not the Azeris'!' Yes, they did march, and they did shout these words." On the one hand, such rallies might be considered provocative; on the other hand, in light of Gorbachev's policy of perestroika, the right to self-determination was perceived to be consonant with a shift in Soviet policy. At least this was how many Armenians interpreted a speech by Gorbachev televised on February 26, 1988.

Whatever the actual motivation for the massacres in Sumgait—hooliganism, as Gorbachev claimed, or a more organized political strategy—there is no moral justification for the carnage. Officially, 31 people were killed, although estimates range as high as 200. According to Samuel Shahmuratian, drawing on 150 interviews with Sumgait survivors,

> For a period of three days in February of 1988, virtually all of Sumgait, a city of over two hundred and fifty thousand, became an arena of mass, unimpeded pogroms of the Armenian population. There were dozens of deaths; in a significant number of cases, the victims were burned alive after beatings and torture. There were hundreds of wounded, many of whom became invalids. There were rapes, including rapes of underage girls. More than two hundred apartments were ravaged, dozens of automobiles were burned or smashed, and dozens of studios, stores, kiosks, and other public property incurred damage. There were thousands of refugees. (*The Sumgait Tragedy,* 1)

The two hundred thousand Armenians living in Baku saw televised reports of events in Sumgait, which was only a short distance away. Many of them had relatives in Sumgait who were eyewitnesses. One Baku resident said, "My husband's relative was living in Sumgait, and he saw everything from his balcony. He saw how a girl was stripped and forced to dance on the street and how they were extinguishing cigarette butts on her skin. He saw it all with his own eyes. When he was telling us about it, he was nervously shaking and crying."

A student from Baku told us about a classmate who frequently traveled by bus to Sumgait. One day this girl was not present in class, and her friend discovered that she was in the hospital. When she went to visit her the next day, she found that the girl was "all beaten up, all black and blue, and she couldn't move from her bed." For nearly two weeks the student visited her friend, whose story gradually unfolded.

She had been traveling to Sumgait when some Azerbaijanis stopped the bus and asked to see everyone's passport. When they discovered that she was Armenian, a woman pulled her by the hair into the aisle and started to kick and beat her. She fainted, and she was thrown out of the bus. Apparently an Azeri couple witnessed her plight, took pity on her, and put her on a bus back to Baku, where she was hospitalized. The injured girl remarked to the student we interviewed, "It's interesting: a Turk beats me up, almost to death, and another Turk, with a good conscience, saves my life."

While visiting her friend in the hospital, the student encountered other casualties of the Sumgait massacres. One person, in particular, affected her: "There was this little boy, his name was Vitalig. I'd say he was in about eighth grade. His mind was totally gone. I found out that, in front of him, the Turks had mutilated his mom and his sister and killed them." She also saw a woman who was recovering from stab wounds to the waist and spoke with another woman whose story deeply troubled her: "There was this young lady, and she told me she had been raped right in front of her dad and beaten up. Right in front of her dad. She said some of those Turks who were watching were neighbors, and they wouldn't do anything. Instead they laughed." And there was a little girl, six or seven years old, who kept crying, "Mom, they're coming." She repeated this over and over and could not be comforted.

Trials of the Sumgait Perpetrators

According to two of the people we interviewed, there were trials, overseen by Russians, of the thugs who carried out the pogroms in Sumgait.

The trial described by one of them started on February 20, 1989, a year after the pogroms. This Armenian woman said that the public prosecutor advised her not to go to testify. "He said that even if they get sentenced, they will not do any time at all, and that going there is worthless and dangerous for us." She also said that evidence kept disappearing and, in addition, that the Russians were themselves being threatened. "The investigators who came from there told us that they were finding notes in their hotel rooms saying, 'Russians, get out.' Important paperwork was disappearing. There was a paper from a gynecologist, Doctor Rashidova, describing the condition my sister was in. That paper disappeared. They guessed that Azeris were stealing important documents, and everyone was advised to lock everything up in safe boxes and photocopy all papers."

On the other hand, apparently the prosecutors were genuinely moved by the accounts and evidence that they encountered. She said that on March 8 they brought them flowers. Eventually, however, the prosecution seemed to grow weary of the case. "In December and January the investigators, too, began to fear going out alone, because they were being attacked. When I was in court in February, the investigators told me that they were counting the days until they could finally leave. They feared for their lives, and all Russians began leaving in December and January."

The story that this woman had to tell the prosecutors described events similar to those experienced by many other Armenians in Sumgait. On February 28 at about noontime, she had seen windows in the neighboring buildings being broken, but a large crowd had not yet gathered. Instead, a group of about twenty people was identifying where Armenians lived, and, she said, "If no one was home when they broke into their apartment, they just threw their belongings out of the windows and burned their homes." Observing this destruction, she said, "We realized that we should stay home and go nowhere. We locked the door, blocked it with the closet, and hid under the bed." When the crowd that developed reached their apartment, their father was the first one to be attacked.

> They ran toward him with an ax. They injured his ear, nose, and chin, although, thank God, those injuries were not serious. However, they injured his back severely, and he is still humpbacked because of that. Some of his bones were broken. When they attacked my dad, my mom jumped between them and my dad, so that she could prevent him from getting hurt, and they struck her head with an ax. She still has numerous scars from that attack.

Her sister then tried to intervene, arguing rationally why they were not to be blamed for what was happening in Nagorno-Karabakh. She told the attackers that all she and her family wanted to do was leave, taking their documents with them, and that they could have everything else. Momentarily, common sense seemed to prevail, but she said some of the people acted as if they were on drugs. "Those standing in the front agreed with us, but those standing in the back yelled at them, asking why they were listening to us and why they were not killing us." She was told that if she would say she was not an Armenian, her life would be spared. Meanwhile, the parents were tied up and dragged into the kitchen. However, a man approached her and told her in Armenian that he was an Azeri but had been forced to join the attacking group. "He untied my mom and my dad and said that while the Azeris were in those two rooms, the hallway was free and they should escape." The neighbors on their floor would not let them in, but those on the third floor welcomed them.

The two sisters, however, were still under attack. "They were beating us with furniture and later I was told that I closed my eyes every time they hit me and covered my face with my hands so that I could not see their faces. I could no longer feel the pain because I was in a state of shock and all that was happening seemed unreal." Then one of the sisters was dragged outside. "Her clothes were torn and she was being beaten severely. It was hard to recognize her afterwards. Her skin was blue, her lips were swollen and bitten through." Observing what was happening, an Azeri neighbor ran to cover her up with a cloth, accusing the attackers of being animals. And, remarkably, this same neighbor later came to apologize for what had occurred. "When those women appeared at our door, my mom did not want to let them in. But they asked her for forgiveness and said that they were sorry about what had happened to our family. They tried to help, and they said that they hid their Armenian neighbors in their apartment."

The woman who told this story said that she also remembered an Azeri intervening on her behalf. She was on the balcony of their apartment when she was being hit, and she remembered seeing a familiar face in front of her. "A man with gray hair was begging them in Azeri not to touch me and to take him instead. He was telling them, 'Please do not touch her. She is our children's teacher.'" She said that he then grabbed an ax and scared them away. Later she remembered who he was, when, during the trial, a young girl and her parents brought her juices and candy. "The girl was a student from my second-grade class, and her parents were elderly, and her father had gray hair. When I saw her father, I realized that he was the one who had come to our apartment. I found out that he had checked hospitals and talked to my neighbors to find out whether I was killed or not."

The other person who spoke of trials after the violence in Sumgait said that they took place in Moscow. The defendants, she said, were "kids," one being sixteen and the other twenty-two. The younger one confessed to burning her husband alive. "I asked him, 'Was it easy for you to do that?' He said, 'Yes.' There was a videotape of him killing people." Apparently the neighbors, looking out their window, had observed him burning her husband alive. When asked whether the neighbors were afraid to testify, she said, "They were afraid. The parents and relatives of those murderers were in the courtroom. They all lived in the same city and nothing would stop them from getting revenge. The parents said that their children were heroes. Only Akhmedov received the death penalty. The rest still had to be 'further investigated.'"

Again, the story this woman told of February 27 and 28 did not differ, except in detail, from those of other Armenians who had been in Sumgait. On the twenty-eighth, her father-in-law reported that his car window had been broken as he was returning from a wedding. That same night they were getting reports of Armenians being killed, but it made no sense to them. "I asked what for, and how could they break into homes and just kill those who lived there." The night of February 28, she said, they got no sleep. They watched their car being turned upside down. They called the militia, but no one responded. "We were seeing things being thrown out of windows and burned. A couple, a husband and a wife, were burned." When the crowd reached their house, they decided to go to the balcony and call for help, but no one responded, so they tried to cross from their balcony to a neighbor's balcony, and in the process our interviewee almost dropped her young daughter.

They then went scurrying up and down the stairs, asking for someone to hide them. Finally, on the fourth floor, neighbors let them in, only to reject them because they feared that the child would cry and attract attention. Meanwhile, they were hearing people shouting, "Cut them, kill them, rape them; we want Armenian blood to flow." Finally they were given temporary shelter, but their host was afraid that if they stayed too long, they would be discovered, and so he asked them to leave, which they did, ending up on the street. By this time there were some soldiers in the area, and they gave them refuge in a protected building. It was there that she discovered that her husband and sister-in-law had been burned alive. Later she learned that her brother-in-law and mother-in-law had also died.

Baku

In November and more intensely in December pogroms started to spread to Baku. One of our interviewees described what she witnessed on December 7, 1988, the day of the earthquake in Armenia: "There is a student housing complex near us, dorms, and when their news program announced the earthquake in Armenia, you can't imagine what they started doing. They started jumping up and down and screaming [in celebration]. And that was the youth. They did not seem human. We have many dorms there, and all of them celebrated; they had fireworks." When queried as to whether she had actually witnessed this, she said, "We could see that from our window. And we could hear their screams." Another survivor said that Azerbaijanis were butchering sheep and barbecuing them right on the streets, singing songs and celebrating that so many Armenians had been killed by the earthquake.

According to Baku refugees whom we interviewed, the attitude toward Armenians rapidly began to deteriorate after the Sumgait massacres, with only intermittent assistance coming from the Soviet army. As one interviewee stated,

> The situation changed drastically. The relationships changed. Azeris became very rude and started treating us with disrespect. Only a few of them were compassionate and even tried to help. The majority were set against us. Everything was different, even at work. It was terrifying. Sometimes it was hard even to leave home. At that time, Armenians were not going anywhere. They could be killed or raped. Anything could be done to them. Some started preparing to leave, and some did not want to believe that it was serious and that it would last.

According to this person, "In March or April, it seemed that some kind of government control, Soviet power, was regained. Later, in June or July of 1988, it ended. There was no more Soviet power; there was nothing. It was a natural anarchy."

Civil disturbances against Armenians continued into 1989. The Armenian cathedral in Baku was burned, and intimidation and hostility toward Armenians intensified. Clearly the cathedral was a symbol of Armenian identity, and it was attacked because of the independence claims of Armenians in Nagorno-Karabakh. Several people we interviewed commented on the fate of the church. "I personally witnessed its destruction. They broke everything inside and blew it up. I cried when I saw it. And every day I would go by that place. They were robbing it and breaking everything inside. It was a wonderful church."

During this period a number of vicious rumors began to circulate about how Azerbaijanis who lived in Armenia were being treated. This disinformation stirred the passions of the general population. An Armenian man who worked at the train station in Baku described the evolution of one such rumor:

> Once, when we were waiting for a train, in June of 1989, a very awful rumor started spreading. They were saying that soon a train would come from Yerevan and bring refugees who were injured: cut into pieces, their noses cut off, their ears cut off, their legs, or their heads. The whole city panicked, and everyone went to that platform waiting for "the train" to come. I went to look, too. The train came, and we saw absolutely healthy people coming out of it. None of them was even scratched.

On his way home he was waiting at a bus stop, and people were talking about "the train" that had just arrived:

> One person was even swearing on the memory of his deceased relatives that he saw how the injured people were brought out of the train, put into the emergency cars, and so on. I couldn't take it anymore, and I told him that he was lying and he was influencing people with his lies. I don't think that they thought of me as an Armenian, because I speak the language [Azeri] very well. I said that I worked on the platform and that I was there when the train arrived. Yes, there were refugees, older people, children, but I had not seen anyone who was injured.

On December 5, 1989, crowds of Azerbaijanis began to threaten Armenians. One of our interviewees said that a group was heading toward his house shouting, "Show us some Armenians; where are the Armenians?" but they turned onto another street before reaching his house. This crowd was stopping buses and pulling out people who were Armenian and beating them. One observer of these actions said that a "crowd instinct" had taken over. In his view, "it was worthless to look for a sense of justice or decency in those animals," even though some Azeris were protesting what was occurring. More than one person told us that the youth in these crowds seemed to be either drunk or on drugs: "They were carrying the Turkish flag—Azerbaijan did not have its own flag at that time. They were walking, yelling, and insulting Armenians. They were like jungle savages."

Beginning on January 13, 1990, a repetition of the pogroms of Sumgait was carried out in Baku against the fifty thousand Armenians who remained. Armenians were pulled out of buses and beaten brutally. One observer of this violence said that several people would gang up on a single Armenian:

> Not one-on-one; about ten or twenty people would attack one person and play with him or her as if with a soccer ball. You can't get close to them, and you can't help. They use whatever they can to torture that person. They use their hands, legs, chains. If a person is lying there all alone, what can he do to protect himself? They murder and then just turn around and leave. Often strangers would ask them, "Why are you beating him or her? Enough!"

Such sadism is difficult to comprehend, especially in view of the rather harmonious relations that had existed between Armenians and Azerbaijanis in Baku. However, the civil anarchy that evolved against Armenians was apparently fueled by implicit approval from respected individuals. For example, one interviewee remarked, "There was a writer who wrote mainly for children, and all of his works were nice and kind. Suddenly, . . . he appeared on television and declared that all people whose last name ended in *ian* must leave and be fired from their jobs." Another interviewee similarly noted the effect of the media on fueling the carnage against Armenians:

> The Azerbaijanis, in groups of five or six people, were going into houses where they knew Armenians lived. When they found a woman there, they raped her; when they found some men, they beat them almost to death. No one could protest against them. No one defended Armenians because they had heard on TV that they were free to do anything they wanted to Armenians. They would stop some cars, and if the driver was Armenian, they would turn the car over, beat the driver, kill him, and burn the car. In the stores, if the salesperson suspected that the buyer was Armenian, she would refuse to sell any bread to that person.

As Armenians attempted to flee the pogroms, they continued to be assaulted. A survivor of these events observed the following from the window of a train bathroom in which he had locked himself.

> I waited there for the train to leave. I could see how the Azerbaijanis were literally burning people. They were pouring gasoline over them and burning them. They were going into the train, dragging out people, checking their passports. I have no idea who gave them the right to do so. . . .
> All of them were dragged out without any regard for their age or gender. Women, older people, younger people were all dragged out of the train. The Azerbaijanis beat them up and burned them and their belongings. There

was one big fire into which everything was thrown. I saw that fire with my own eyes. People were pushed into it after being beaten.

When asked whether Soviet soldiers were there, he replied that the crowds were so "mad" that the soldiers did not dare get close to what was occurring. In his view, the scene was analogous to animals tearing apart a prey that they have captured.

Apparently there was widespread conversation in the streets about forcing Armenians out of Azerbaijan. Violence was the form of intimidation, and Armenians throughout the city were debating when and how they should leave, even though they were in a state of disbelief that this was actually happening.

> On January 12 [1990], the whole city was talking about a massacre scheduled for the next day. I was listening to people talking about it and could not believe it. What massacres? Why? When I went to the city on the thirteenth, people were saying that the massacres would be in the evening, and I still did not believe it. However, when I went there on the fourteenth and took a bus, I overheard a conversation among some Azeris; my Azeri is very good, and I could understand them very well. One person asked what had happened yesterday, had they killed any Armenians? I found out that many Armenians had been killed that day. They were thrown from the second and third floors.

On returning home this person said that he observed a woman resisting attack; she tried to keep her assailants from entering her house. "They broke in and threw her down from the second floor."

On January 18 he came home and found that the doors of his apartment were broken. "And inside, there were several Azeris standing in a group. All that I had, the TV and the furniture, was missing. The apartment was empty. I understood everything and decided to be careful, because if I protested, they would just finish me. Militia would never help in those cases." Describing what then transpired, he said, "I walked into the apartment and they said, 'You see, you have to leave.' I said, 'Of course I will leave, but please give me at least my documents.' They said they would not give them to me. Finally, they gave me my passport. And they did not give me the rest of my documents. They threatened me and I had to leave."

On January 19, 1990, a state of emergency was declared, and 20,000 Soviet troops were sent in to quell the riots against the Armenians. According to one report, 93 Azerbaijanis and 29 Russian soldiers died in street skirmishes. After the Baku pogroms, Armenians from all over Azerbaijan fled—some to Armenia and others to Moscow and other places where they could find work. Apparently the Russians even provided planes to transport Armenians to Yerevan. Other individuals went by train. Ironically, some of the Sumgait refugees who left after the February uprisings ended up in Spitak, Gyumri, and Vanadzor, cities that were hard hit by the earthquake. Thus, they faced two major traumatic events within a single year.

A few Armenians were able to sell some of their possessions before leaving, and even their houses, but others were not so fortunate. For example, one person said he thought that he had sealed a deal to sell his house to a young married couple who had just graduated from college. Once they saw the violence escalating against Armenians, however, they asked why they should buy it when the house was going to be vacated anyway. It appears, at least according to one person we interviewed, that the houses of fleeing Armenians were being reserved for Azerbaijanis who were leaving Armenia, which precluded any official sale of Armenian-owned houses. Refugees from Azerbaijan often arrived in Armenia, therefore, with almost no possessions. Furthermore, many of them spoke only haltingly in Armenian. To compound the tragedy, they arrived in time to experience the terrible winter conditions that prevailed for the next four years.

Political Analysis

Our interviews with refugees from Azerbaijan clearly indicate that there was a strong division of opinion regarding the violence against Armenians and the effort to force them out of the country. Neighbors and friends of Armenians were often horrified by what was happening. When direct violence occurred against their Armenian neighbors, they often provided temporary refuge, but Azeris were also often fearful that the marauding crowd would attack them if they were found to be sheltering Armenians.

A pattern of anarchy developed that allowed the baser elements of the human personality to emerge. So long as law and order are enforced, inclinations toward rape, murder, and sadism are held in check. But when individuals know that their actions will bring no consequences, some people, whether they are in Los Angeles or Baku, exhibit the underside of human nature. In Sumgait and Baku, this demonic element of human nature was magnified by group agitation. Few people, by themselves, would have pursued wanton violence, but group fervor clearly developed—a type of mob hysteria—which encouraged people to commit atrocities that would have been unthinkable had they been premeditated. An interviewee from Baku gave an example of this mob psychology. "One day I saw a riot. A mob of Azeris walking. They were mostly young men and women, just screaming. The men had knives and the women were screaming, and they were screaming so hard that they were getting the guys to be even more aggressive." And the government apparently tolerated, if it did not approve of, the activities that were calculated to generate mob enthusiasm to attack Armenians.

> There is a big square near the main government building [in Baku]. From November 17 to December 5 [1989], the meetings were held there. They even had tents there. They had food and drinks. When they were dismissed, it was something terrible. They were going from one Armenian house to another. One of our relatives, my cousin, was killed at that time. They broke into his house and, not using a knife or any other weapon, they just beat him to death.

Obviously, a criminal element exists in every society, and a very small number of people commit atrocities that shock the public consciousness. In the pogroms in Azerbaijan, however, hundreds of people engaged in mob activity.

In addition to whatever satisfaction might have been derived from savage attacks on individuals, there was the selfish urge to steal other people's goods: television sets, furniture, jewelry, and other items of value. During the 1992 riots in Los Angeles, we personally observed ordinary citizens walking out of shoe stores with boxes of stolen items. In fact, there was a carnival atmosphere because the police were nowhere to be seen. In large part, this is precisely what occurred in Sumgait and Baku. For a while, there was no attempt to enforce law and order. Not only did the local police appear to sympathize with what was occurring, but the Russian army did not act aggressively in Sumgait until it was too late, and in Baku their power seems to have waned by 1990.

At some level the attackers' violence against Armenians was not only fueled by the conflict in Nagorno-Karabakh but also justified as support for their motherland. According to one interviewee, demonstrations occurring in Baku were not only against the Armenians, they were also against Jews and Russians. "Often they were holding demonstrations and carrying big signs saying, 'Armenians get out of Baku!' 'Jews be prepared!' 'Russians be our slaves.'" What was missing was any acknowledgment of the civil rights of individuals, due process of law, and an ability to distinguish between loyal Armenian residents of Azerbaijan and Armenians engaged in a liberation struggle in Nagorno-Karabakh. Instead, there was reversion to a primitive morality of "us" against "them."

Unfortunately, this mentality had strong parallels with previous patterns of sadistic violence against Armenians, including rape, physical disfigurement, and torture, that occurred in the 1915 genocide. In addition, the festive celebration of Armenian deaths was common to the events of both 1915 and 1988–90, and other parallels exist between the two time periods, such as Armenians being forced to abandon or sell household articles at a fraction of their real value.

In spite of the similarities noted, there are also substantial differences between the 1915 genocide and the events of 1988–90. During the genocide, news of the massacres and deportations in various provinces spread rather slowly, by word of mouth, so it was not immediately apparent that a coordinated plan of extermination was unfolding. In contrast, technology allowed almost instant communication and linkage of events in Sumgait, Baku, Yerevan, Stepanakert, and other towns. Technology had other effects as well: both airplanes and trains helped refugees to get away from Azerbaijan in a way that was not possible during the genocide. Another difference is that refugees had a host country to which they could flee (i.e., Armenia), which they lacked in 1915. Yet another difference is that whatever role the Soviet government may have played in fostering the recent pogroms, it also had the power to stop them, which was not true of any single power during World War I except for, perhaps, Turkey's ally, Germany.

Although there are parallels between the genocide and the pogroms in Azerbaijan, there may be more direct parallels between the massacres of 1894–96 in Turkey, as well as those of 1909, and the pogroms of 1988–90 in Azerbaijan. For one thing, the events in Baku and Sumgait cannot technically be called genocide, but, even more important, the methodology of the 1988–90 pogroms is more similar to that of the pre-1915 period. The 1894–96 massacres were typically rather localized and only lasted a day or two, paralleling the Sumgait and Baku pogroms. They seemed intended to send a message to the Armenians about their role and place as a minority population, rather than actually to exterminate the entire population. The 1909 massacres in Adana had some of the same qualities: they were a vicious reaction to Armenian claims for equal treatment and rights, not an attempt to kill all Armenians living in the region. The motives of the recent pogroms may have been more complex, depending on whether the focus is the Soviet government—which may have used the massacres to send a message to the Armenian SSR regarding independence and the unification of Armenia and Nagorno-Karabakh—or the aim of the perpetrators of the direct violence, which seemed to reflect an older spirit of nationalistic racism.

When we asked refugees to reflect on the pogroms they had experienced, several people made a direct comparison to the Armenian genocide of 1915. Others referred to the slaughter of fifteen thousand Armenians who were put to the sword in Baku in 1918. Genocide comparisons would probably have been even more overt in our interviews except for the fact that many Armenians living in Baku and Sumgait were highly assimilated. Some had married Azerbaijanis, and many upwardly mobile parents sent their children to Russian schools, which they thought would contribute to their advancement, rather than to Armenian schools, which they feared would marginalize their children. Consequently, Armenian history was often known more through family memories than through formal education.

One cannot easily explain why three hundred and fifty thousand Armenians would leave their homes, possessions, and childhood memories, except that they feared a repetition of events that had too frequently marked them as a survivor people. However horrific the pogroms were, it is also true that a relatively small number of people were killed: 31 in Sumgait and 160 in Baku, according to official counts (although these may be considerable underestimates). Such a massive reaction by the Armenian population was certainly based partly on their fear concerning their current situation. In addition, however, deep in their historical memory was a conviction, articulated in the words of one interviewee, that *never again* would Armenians be "lambs for the slaughter."

The social and political conditions faced by Armenians living in Azerbaijan paralleled too closely the context of previous massacres and genocides for Armenians not to be alarmed when the pogroms in Sumgait broke out. More specifically, the following comparisons exist between the recent pogroms against the Armenian population and the previous threats to their existence: (1) Armenians were a minority population in both Azerbaijan and Turkey and were thus clearly identifiable as objects of persecution; (2) Armenians were more upwardly mobile than the majority population; hence, they were likely to be the objects of jealousy and envy; (3) the overarching political conditions were unstable in both the Soviet Union and the Ottoman Empire—and revolutionary change is a prerequisite for most massacres and genocides; and (4) Armenians were made scapegoats for political events beyond the borders of the country in which they lived.

We have wondered what the fate of the Armenian population would have been had there still been Armenians living in Baku and Sumgait between 1993 and 1994, when the war in Nagorno-Karabakh began to turn against the Azerbaijanis. It is possible that a new genocide against the Armenian population was avoided because large numbers of Armenians from Azerbaijan emigrated after the massacres of 1988–90.

3

Fighting for Survival

The War of Independence in Nagorno-Karabakh

In August of 1993 we decided to take the research team to Nagorno-Karabakh. Our research assistants had been documenting the results of the blockade on Armenia, which was a direct consequence of the Republic of Armenia's support of the liberation struggle in Nagorno-Karabakh. And so it was time to visit Stepanakert, the capital city of this Armenian enclave that had attempted to maintain its ethnic identity within the boundaries of Azerbaijan since 1921, when Stalin ceded it to the Azeris.

The appointed morning arrived, and since some members of our group were frightened about the prospects of the journey, we went to the Artsakh headquarters in Yerevan to inquire about the safety of the trip. Nothing could be guaranteed, but we were told that the Lachin Corridor road was open, and so six members of our research team climbed into the rented van, along with photographer Jerry Berndt, our son, and the person who was later to translate all of our interviews, Arpi Haleblian. In the back of the van we had extra cans of gasoline, along with a huge pile of lavash bread and some other food. As we headed out of Yerevan, one

Bullet-pocked cross marks the entrance to the Lachin Corridor.

of our research assistants asked if we could stop for a moment at a relative's house, and a few minutes later she returned with a fifty-pound sack of grain for family members in Stepanakert. To say that we were loaded down was an understatement, because the driver had also insisted on bringing along a friend.

The drive to Goris, the last major town before crossing into the disputed Lachin Corridor, was beautiful, passing through rolling mountains and farmland composed as much of rocks as of soil. The view of Goris as we looked down on it from a winding road was postcard perfect, with tile-roofed houses perched on the sides of hills that spilled into a small

Every home in the Lachin Corridor was destroyed.

valley. We had a leisurely lunch in an all-but-deserted restaurant and then headed for the border.

The first sight that greeted us as we crossed a small river and entered the Lachin Corridor was a hand-painted cross on a rock wall. As we got out of the car to stretch our legs, we saw that the cross was pocked with bullet holes, obviously put there by people who disagreed that this was Christian territory. Within a very short distance it was clear that this highway connecting Armenia with Nagorno-Karabakh had been bitterly fought over. Recently it had been occupied by Azeris, thus making Nagorno-Karabakh a geographical island disconnected from the Republic of Armenia. Every house had been torched or hit by shells, rendering the area uninhabitable. When we stopped to examine some of these structures, we stayed on the road for fear of stepping on land mines planted by defending soldiers.

We pulled into the main square in Stepanakert shortly before dusk and, with our logistics coordinator, headed to a large hotel where we assumed we could stay for the night. Quite predictably, although it had never occurred to us, the hotel was filled to overflowing with refugees from Martakert and other Armenian regions that had been occupied by

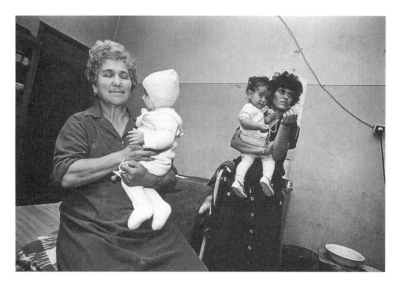

Every room in the largest hotel in Stepanakert was filled with refugees.

Azeri troops. Each room held at least one family, sometimes two, and there was no room for a van full of tired passengers. Fortunately, one of our research assistants, the one who had brought the sack of grain, said that she would call her uncle and see if he had any suggestions. After a few tense moments and several telephone calls on his part, we were told to head for the children's hospital. They had some unoccupied beds, and we could stay there.

Like every other building in town, the hospital had no glass in the windows. All of the panes had been blown out by exploding bombs or shells that had rained down on the city from nearby Shushi, which was located in a position from which Russian Grad missiles were very effective. Plastic sheets had been tacked up to replace the glass. The hospitality of the people, however, more than compensated for the accommodations—we slept in beds that sagged in the middle, and we were pleased that we had brought along a water purification pump, because we could see debris floating in the bathtub that served as a reservoir should the electricity fail.

The next day our research assistants fanned out to begin interviewing people, and we headed for the military hospital. It was a clean and well-managed facility, but we were depressed by the knot of women—

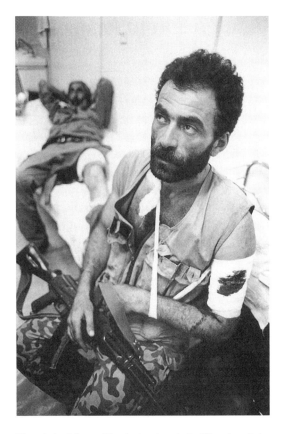

Wounded soldier waiting for treatment at military hospital
in Stepanakert.

some with infants in their arms—that gathered every time a military hel-
icopter brought in the wounded, obviously looking for a husband or
brother who was coming home. In the hospital waiting room, we saw
soldiers in military fatigues, still holding rifles on their laps. They had
been patched up by field medics and were here for surgery or more sus-
tained treatment.

Some of the soldiers were carried in on stretchers, and we saw more
than one, in the short time we were there, with serious head and face
wounds. One image, in particular, stuck in our minds: a man lay naked

on his back with two short stumps for legs that were bandaged after recent amputations. His head was also wrapped with gauze. Later in Yerevan, we visited a hospital that was fitting men, and even a few women, with prosthetic devices. This was the fruit of a war and a territory strewn with land mines that, by the time of the cease-fire on May 12, 1994, had claimed as many as twenty thousand lives and left more than a million people homeless, both Armenians and Azerbaijanis.

Stepanakert was as starved for fuel as Yerevan. We didn't see a single private car being driven while we were there. Every resource was reserved for the military effort. Fortunately, my wife and I were invited to stay with a government information officer and his wife, who was a physician, on the second and subsequent nights, and they extended extraordinary hospitality to us. However, even this well-appointed house had holes in the walls, evidence of shrapnel from exploding bombs. Our interviews revealed that, prior to taking Shushi from the Azeris (a historic Armenian city from which the Azeris were deploying missiles), families had been spending a great deal of time in underground bomb shelters.

We also went back to the refugee-filled hotel and interviewed families. Very few men were there. Most of them were defending their village or fighting on the front lines. Tragically, many of the women were young widows who had pinned photographs of their husbands to the walls. And there were also grandparents taking care of children, either because their mothers had died or, in a few instances, were fighting alongside the men in the army. One strong-looking elderly woman with two young children under her command showed us a bulging sac on her head the size of an egg—the result of being struck during the invasion of her village. We also chatted with a soldier on the steps of the hotel who was home on leave for a few days, and he pulled from his wallet the picture of a good friend who had recently been killed. Indeed, throughout the streets of Stepanakert, Shushi, and Yerevan, black banners waved over the streets bearing the names and ages of people who had paid the price of the independence struggle.

Tragedy, as always, occurred on both sides of the conflict. We visited a group of Azeri women and child hostages who said that they had been captured by Armenian soldiers during a wedding celebration. And we also briefly met two Russian mercenary pilots whose planes had been shot down by Armenians during bombing raids. In addition to these Russians, there were Afghan mujahideen and Ukraine mercenaries that the Azeri government had hired. Many of the Azeri young men who had

Many hotel rooms occupied by refugees in Stepanakert had
photographs of fathers and husbands who were defending
the homeland.

been drafted into the army saw no purpose or mission behind the war
effort. One Armenian soldier we interviewed said that these soldiers in
their late teens and twenties sometimes cried like children when they were
captured.

Origins of the War

The moral claim to Nagorno-Karabakh by Armenians rested on the argument of self-determination, while the counterargument by the Azer-

baijan government was that of territorial integrity. Armenians had lived in this mountainous area for over two thousand years, and when the region was given by Stalin to Azerbaijan in 1921 it was well over 90 percent Armenian. By 1988 the region had been deliberately diluted to 75 percent Armenian by aggressive policies to settle Azeris in the territory. An individual we interviewed said, "There were a lot of Azeris coming to Karabakh, doctors and engineers, buying homes, and had you allowed them to do this, within ten years they would have crowded all the Armenians out." But the Armenian spirit had never left the Nagorno-Karabakh people, and in 1987–88, prompted by Mikhail Gorbachev's policy of perestroika, residents sent thousands of letters to the Kremlin requesting independence from Azerbaijan. One person we interviewed described the influence of Gorbachev's policies as follows: "When Gorbachev announced his glasnost program, it sort of woke us up. We realized that we needed and wanted democracy. You see, all we had done prior to this time was work and allow the Azeris to eat. We worked hard, and they ate. Now we realized that we ought to fight for our own rights."

Another person described the demonstrations that took place in Stepanakert. "There were ten to thirty thousand of us in the main plaza, the town square. Gorbachev had talked and stirred us all up. The people shouted, 'Unite Karabakh with Armenia.'" The demonstrations provoked a collective sense of political ecstasy. For the first time in seventy years the feeling of freedom was in the air, and people were ready to embrace it. An older woman remembered, "I was absolutely happy and enraptured with our movement. I went, I participated, and I was very happy. I remember shouting and singing, and even today my friends come up to me and blame me, remembering how much I shouted and screamed and was happy with independence." She then reflected, "I was and I still am." And she was not alone. Another woman said,

> You know, in Armenia there are three million Armenians, and I would say that during the independence movement and the Karabakh movement we had some two million people out in the plaza, out in the center of the town. Everyone was there. I remember I used to work and then go home, and then come and participate in the meetings. At least twice a week; I tried [to go] twice a week. Many times with my husband and other times with friends. I was enthusiastic. I was involved. I wanted to come and hear and know what was going on.

On February 20, 1988, Nagorno-Karabakh adopted a resolution to transfer governance from Soviet Azerbaijan to Soviet Armenia. This action led to anti-Armenian pogroms in the Azerbaijani town of Sumgait, described in the previous chapter, and at the same time to massive demonstrations in the streets of Yerevan in favor of the resolution. On June 13, 1988, the Supreme Soviet of the Azerbaijani SSR predictably denied the application of the Nagorno-Karabakh Assembly to unite with Armenia. On June 15 of the same year, Armenia's Supreme Soviet approved Nagorno-Karabakh's proposal. Finally, on December 10, 1991, Nagorno-Karabakh Armenians held a referendum calling for independence that was overwhelmingly approved.

Drawing on the Russian arms market, as well as arms captured from Azeri troops, Nagorno-Karabakh put together a potent fighting force. Armenians, however, felt under siege. In 1992 Azeri forces occupied almost half of Nagorno-Karabakh's territory—the entire northern area that included Martakert. Armenians were in an untenable military position and launched an all-out offensive in the spring of 1993, finally taking the Kelbajar region of Azerbaijan on March 27 (this was an area that separated Nagorno-Karabakh from Armenia). They also wanted to neutralize forces in the Azeri town of Fizuli, as well as other regions, in order to protect themselves from constant bombardment. During all of this time the president of the fledgling Republic of Armenia, which itself had become independent on September 23, 1991, maintained an official position of non-engagement in the Nagorno-Karabakh conflict, although this was a bit of political fiction, since the cemeteries of Armenia were filling up with the graves of men slain in battle in Nagorno-Karabakh.

We can verify the participation of volunteers from Armenia. In 1993 we were buying *rojig* (walnuts covered with grape syrup) at a roadside stand outside of Yerevan when a middle-aged man, a physical education instructor dressed in military fatigues, insisted that we follow his car to a cemetery a few miles away. What he wanted to show us was the place where already a dozen of his battalion of fifty had been buried. Presumably he was a "volunteer," but surely Armenians were also supplying aid to their brethren in Nagorno-Karabakh, in spite of insisting that the conflict was between the Armenians of Nagorno-Karabakh and the Azerbaijani government.

War is an ugly business, whichever side has the moral high ground. Because of the pogroms against the Armenian population living in Azerbaijan, more than three hundred thousand Armenians had become refugees, fleeing to Yerevan, resettling in the Lachin Corridor, searching out a new life in Moscow, or going elsewhere. Likewise, about one hundred and fifty thousand Azeris left Armenia, along with approximately forty thousand from Nagorno-Karabakh, and they took over houses abandoned by Armenians in Baku and Sumgait, settled elsewhere in Azerbaijan, or took up residence in refugee camps. In addition, the thousands of Azeris forced out of Kelbajar, Fizuli, Agdam, and Lachin (including some who fled to northern Iran, which has large Azeri settlements) ended up living in miserable conditions.

A key player in the conflict was Russia. Originally, there seemed to be a sentiment of punishing both Nagorno-Karabakh and Armenia for their independence drives. Russian troops sometimes led the way for the invading Azerbaijani army. For example, one person said, "Russian tanks came into our village and started firing. They were very close to us; the tanks were just five meters away from me. Right after that the Turkish [Azeri] army walked in." Later, however, it appeared that Russian domination was best achieved by supporting both Azerbaijan and Nagorno-Karabakh, playing one side against the other and thereby keeping both weak. People said, for example, that the Russian army warned them to leave, stating that the Azerbaijani army was coming, but the Russians did not fire on them. Ultimately, Russia sided with Armenia, probably for two reasons. First, Armenia is an important buffer between Russia and Turkey, which some fear might still harbor the goal of a pan-Turkic empire. Second, Russia has a strong interest in Caspian Sea oil, and keeping Baku in a weakened position is ultimately in Russia's self-interest. Hence, the cease-fire since 1994 has held because of the presence of Russian peacekeepers and the threat of Russian troop involvement if the conflict should reignite. Nevertheless, one cannot underestimate the resolve of the people of Nagorno-Karabakh to maintain control of the territory they currently occupy.

Relations before the War

Many of the people we interviewed reported that prior to 1988 they had cordial relationships with Azeris who lived in their town or village. One woman said, "We got along very well. There was no problem. We lived peacefully together. Our kids played with one another. We celebrated things together." Another Armenian remembered befriending an Azeri woman who was turned away from a hotel because she did not have the proper documentation. "She was tired and hungry. We fed her and we housed her. So, our relations with Turks were normal." Nevertheless, there was very little intermarriage, and when it did occur there was inevitably a certain awkwardness about where loyalties ultimately rested. As one person said, "There was one Turkish woman married to an Armenian, but he was looked down on as a traitor. But the relations between the Armenians and Turks were okay in that we did buying and selling."

The one complaint that we heard consistently was that Armenians did not enjoy complete freedom. One woman said regarding the educational system, "They forced us to bring in Azeri history. We had to teach our Armenian children Azeri history! We had to cut short on our Armenian history." She also said that there was sometimes prejudice against Armenian students: "We Armenians studied hard. But would you believe that our Azeri instructor was mean and wanted to fail us?" She added, however, that "there was an Azeri student who fought for us and said, 'How come they are not getting good grades and I am?' Anyway, we did very well on our finals and we got very good grades. I got top grades, actually." Another person said, "Azeris did not let us have Armenian books from Yerevan. All the books that we got were from Baku, and if there was any mention of the genocide, that book was prohibited so that it never got to the students. We had no permission to spread Armenian literature." In short, there seemed to be a deliberate attempt to stifle the creation of Armenian consciousness. Furthermore, coincident with the beginning of the independence movement, the Azerbaijani government became more dominant. "He [the president of Azerbaijan] wanted the Armenian schools to teach the Azeri language, and slowly he was trying to penetrate into every corner of the Armenian community and increase the number of Azeris everywhere so that we would eventually become a minority. We felt it. Our leaders felt it." Resettlement is, of course, an obvious strategy followed by any dominant group that is trying to neutralize the political power of another nationality (e.g., the Israeli settlements in Palestine).

In Shushi, Armenians were not allowed to hold top government positions. A resident of Nagorno-Karabakh said, "There was no intelligentsia. Those positions were taken by Azeris. Armenians had no chance except to work with their hands. The only high position that an Armenian could get was to be the secretary of the mayor." When the independence movement started, outright discrimination began in Shushi. A medical doctor said that for twelve years she had worked peacefully with her colleagues, but on May 16, 1988, the fourteen Armenians working in her hospital were all fired.

Armenian church on hill in Shushi, in which Grad missiles were stored by Azeri soldiers before Armenians recaptured the city.

> I had a conference with the chief medical doctor of the hospital and I was all alone in the room and other Azeri doctors came and I just wanted answers and I wanted to talk to them, but they were very mean to me. I was all alone and they were using foul language to me and about my country and my countrymen—Armenians in general. And this was extremely unpleasant.

She said that she was so upset by what was happening that "I all of a sudden got courage and I made a fist and knocked on the table and said, 'If you had only said these words to me, I could have taken it. But since you are saying all these words against my nation, I can't take it.'" And she lectured them, saying that Shushi belonged to the Armenians, and that they would lose this city because of their actions against the Armenians. And, in fact, when Shushi was taken by the Armenians on May 18, 1992, she returned two days later to keep a promise she had made: "I had vowed that [when the Armenians conquered Shushi] I would walk there by foot and light a candle in the church."

As the independence movement gained momentum, relations between Armenians and Azeris became increasingly polarized—especially after the pogroms against Armenians who were living in Azerbaijan. "We were close physically to the Turks. Our village was only about five hundred meters away from theirs. We had good relations with them. But when the Sumgait incident took place, slowly things started to get bad here as well. We started to steal their sheep, their donkeys. They stole our sheep, our donkeys." The Azeris abducted a young Armenian man from this village and killed him in revenge for the robberies. Elsewhere the Armenians killed an Azeri doctor in retaliation for the burning of homes by Azerbaijanis.

> It was after the Sumgait affair that they became ferocious, and they started pillaging and killing, and confiscating everything they could. Within three days they got to our village. Our village was very rich in every way—our soil, our land. So they just confiscated things—they burned two homes only; the rest they just took. They killed an Armenian man from our village. His son was so angry he said, "For revenge, I will go and kill a doctor, a Turk doctor," and he did.

A woman from Martakert said that the "war ruined everything." She indicated that, prior to independence, Armenians and Azeris enjoyed good relations. A university student we interviewed echoed the same sentiment. "Yes, we have always had good relations with Azeris, but in school and as neighbors. But once the meetings [related to independence] started, animosity started right with it."

Initially, there was a festive spirit that drove the independence movement. A woman said, "When I was in Martakert I participated in the movement, and there were so many people who took part. We took off from our work and took part in the demonstrations and the movement, and we were all for Karabakh to be under Armenia rather than under the Turks. You see, the Turks were pressuring us so much. They wanted us to forget that we were Armenians. They didn't want anything to do with Armenia, the Armenian language, or Armenians. They wanted us all to become Azeri, Turk." The same spirit motivated people to defend their towns and villages when attacks came. A woman said, "Most of those who went to the front were optimistic. They were real heroes. They were protecting their town, villages, people." Another woman said, "Yes, we had fedayeen, the volunteers. They got organized, and they were a good resistance group, and the people supported them every way they could, and they were very well organized, and they were able to defend themselves and fight against the Turks. My husband was sixty-seven years old, and he wanted to participate. He was so anxious to defend."

Bombing and Atrocities

There may have been atrocities on both sides of this conflict; we are not in a position to make a judgment regarding possible Armenian attacks on Azerbaijanis. But certainly barbaric acts were committed against the Armenians. From Shushi bombs rained down on the defenseless city of Stepanakert until May 18, 1992, when Armenians managed the nearly impossible feat of scaling the walls of the city and took it over. Prior to that time, however, families became accustomed to living in bomb shelters. "We stayed there some eighteen days. There was bombing. Every time there was bombing, we would go in shelters, underground. When the bombing would stop, we would come out. It was on and off, on and off. They would bomb one day and then move on, start the next day, you know." One woman described the actual condition of the shelter.

> We had to run away because the bombing had increased in Stepanakert. You see, we had our own home, but we could not stay there because of the bombing. So we had to hide underground. There were about two hundred and fifty of us in a small room, a hundred meters long and forty meters wide, that had no windows, just a door. So it was not particularly comfortable, but it was safe.

Another woman recalled their shelter as follows: "There were four rooms, and in each room there were five families, all with children. Yes, we were crowded." On the other hand, life went on in these shelters. One couple even got married. "This was a fedayee wedding, and only people who were around were able to come [rather than the extended family and friends]." Also, she said, "they didn't have a wedding gown. Just plain clothes. Nice clothes, though." And, of course, some women gave birth in the shelters.

When bombs were not falling, people would head back to their homes and prepare food. A mother said, "You see, we had to make bread for the kids. We had to go to our homes and cook between the times of bombing so that we could stay alive." And sometimes there were extended lulls in the bombing.

> One day we were watching TV and my son was playing outside, and all of a sudden, after two months of complete quiet, the bombing started all over again. It scared us stiff, and right away I thought of my son. I had to run out, and I saw our two-story home just crashing down. As I was running and crying for my son, I saw injured neighbors and men with all kinds of injuries—one man's internal organs were showing. I saw this young bride

Armenian fedayeen in Shushi enjoying a break from the front.

fall down with her throat cut. I saw this old woman under the ruins, and she was dead. I was running and looking for my son.

She found her son, but eighteen of her neighbors died, and after telling this story, she said, "It was awful, just awful. As I am telling you this story right now I am reliving the nightmare. It was just unbelievably tragic. Unbelievable. Awful. Terrible."

Bombing is an impersonal form of attack in which the perpetrator only later may witness the results on property or human targets. But there were also atrocities committed firsthand that defy the boundaries of civilized exchange between peoples. For example, two Armenian men were tied to trees opposite each other—one a fedayee and another an old man. "It was terrible because they cut his ears first. They beat him up. Then they cut him up. They were so cruel and merciless. They picked his heart out, this young man's heart, and said, 'This is what we are going to do to the Armenians.'"

Sometimes family members were singled out for attack, even though they were not directly involved in the conflict. For example, a woman said that her father was beaten because his son was a fedayee. Another woman said that when the Azeris attacked her village, she fled with her children to a neighboring village and stayed overnight. Many of the men stayed behind to defend their homes, and in the morning she and her husband ventured back to see what had happened.

> When we returned we saw young men killed—blood all over the place. Young women had been raped and killed. Homes burned. . . . And then we went to a friend's house. There was this twenty-one-year-old boy whose head was cut off. His father lay there on the floor [next to him] in a pool of blood. He was cut open. It was just dreadful. What happened was that those who stayed behind were slaughtered. There were no arms to fight back with, and all the houses that remained were looted.

Armenian villages were often attacked intermittently, so that people sometimes simply stumbled upon terrible situations:

> The bus stopped and I wanted to know what was going on, and they told us the village was being captured or being filled with Azeri soldiers and they were killing and ruining everything. Sure enough, our bus went to our village, and as we approached—we were almost there—we saw the fighting going on. So many wounded. So many killed. The Azeris were trying to take over. So we had no choice but to run away ourselves. The men were not able to help us because they were busy trying to help the wounded and the dead.

Another interviewee gave a more tragic account of a bus trip, which took her family members close to the border with Azerbaijan:

> So they attacked the bus, and they killed the bus driver, and they killed six people in the bus, including my cousin, my aunt's daughter, and another woman who was young and had two children. They tortured these six people and killed them. The rest were able to run away and hide in the forest until they were saved. Would you believe that I was going to go on that very bus to visit my parents? My brother went on it; he was saved, and he was an eyewitness to this awful thing that happened.

Fleeing to Safety

Many people were caught relatively unaware when their village was invaded. One woman said that she was baking bread at the time:

> There was lots of food in the house, but my husband said, "Don't worry about bread and baking. You've got to flee." I hadn't realized it was that serious. I thought, "How can Turks kill us?" I mean, "What's going on? I'm going to make my bread." Anyway, my husband tried to get all the women to flee to the valley. There was a valley next to our village. He

was trying to get us all there, so that we would be safe. But they got my husband and they shot him. I didn't see that at the time. All I remember is that I didn't find him and kept asking for him, and they said he was shot but he wasn't killed. I finally found him. He had fallen into a ditch and I saw him. He was bloodied and I cried. I took water and washed his wound. Ten centimeters of his foot bone was gone.

People fled with only the clothes on their back and a little food. Often, they were aided by people in villages that had not yet been attacked, as in the following case:

> Four of us were fleeing together. Everyone was fleeing on his or her own. We walked until it was night and we reached a village, and we stayed there overnight. Then we walked again to the next village. Finally we made it to Stepanakert. Everywhere we went, people would go to us. They would clothe us and feed us and give us whatever we needed. Those villagers were very friendly, but now they themselves have fled as well because the enemy reached them.

At other times, however, people thought only of their own safety; it was simply a mad scramble for survival. One woman remembered, for example, how a mother with an infant had to beg for help. "I gave her something and she just hugged me. It was tragic. I didn't have money, but I gave her what I had." Elderly people were also disadvantaged, having difficulty walking long distances for several days. And children sometimes were instructed to leave on such short notice that they didn't even put on shoes for the journey. A mother said, "No one had prepared. No one was ready to leave. No one knew what to take with them as they left." Another mother described the chaos that surrounded their evacuation:

> So here we are trying to escape the enemy, but kids are crying, people are confused, we don't know what to do. All of a sudden we see my husband in his car passing by. I know he is returning from Stepanakert to our village. We shout, but he doesn't see us, and he goes to the village. Apparently he went there and went to our house, and there was no one. He asked around, and people said that many people had run to the river without taking anything from their houses.

The Azeris made a concerted effort to force people to abandon their homes, as recounted by this woman who lost her husband in the war but survived with her two children.

> I remember one day when there was fighting for twelve hours, nonstop. We did not flee. We stayed in our village during this time. Turks came by with

a bigger force and fired at us at random. They burned homes, and lots of people died. We had to flee. My mom left afterwards, and she saw a lot of evidence of torture, like one man with his head cut off and another man burned—people tortured to death. The Azeris were very ferocious. My father's aunt was killed. We had to flee, but I returned and got food for the kids because our house was full of food.

In addition, she baked bread for her husband and his friends, who were attempting to defend the village.

Even the animals suffered in this war. One couple moved their children to a neighboring village where they thought they would be safe, but they stayed behind to see what would happen and to care for their farm. The husband reported that he and his wife were hiding in a trench out of harm's way when she said, "Why don't we get up and feed our animals, poor things. They'll starve." So they went to tend to their livestock. But after a few minutes they realized it wasn't safe. "We had to run back into the trench. We realized that we had to flee. It was just getting fierce and people were dying right and left."

On the other hand, the journey to safety was sometimes relatively comfortable, as it was for this family that traveled by automobile:

> We were told to leave in the middle of the night. It was cold and raining, but we had to leave. I was crying. I dressed the children and made sure they were all warm. I put blankets around all of them, and we were taken to Stepanakert in the car. There we stayed with some friends for three days. Then we came back to our village and stayed in the forest with lots of other refugees. From there my son brought us here to Yerevan.

This family, however, was the exception. Many people fled on foot, such as this group of fifty people who walked for several days until they reached Stepanakert:

> Awful things happened on the way as we were fleeing. There was one pregnant woman, and she couldn't give birth to the baby. She knew that she was not going to make it. She asked her husband to kill her. He killed her and then he killed himself. They both decided on the spot to end their lives rather than go through torture. Another woman with her kids decided to jump into the river and kill herself with her children, because she knew they couldn't make it.

In some ways these scenes resemble accounts of the Armenian genocide and the forced deportation marches. In fact, some people we interviewed made explicit reference to the genocide, especially regarding why, this time, they chose to fight and defend themselves. "So I had these pow-

erful feelings thinking back to 1915. In 1915 Armenians were totally un-
protected, vulnerable, and were hurt by Turks. [But] we are here to defend ourselves, take back our country, our city, and all." Another person called the conflict with Azerbaijan a "second genocide."

> They were attacking us from all three sides, so we had no choice. I remem-
> ber as we were running away to the neighboring village, tanks were coming.
> All our guys just had hand arms, automatic arms to fight back, but they had
> no tanks or anything. Here the Turks were coming with these huge tanks.
> So as I said, we ran to the next village where it was safer, and everyone was
> crying. It was chaos. I thought of our genocide in 1915, and I had read a
> lot of books on it, and it reminded me of it. I said, "This is a second geno-
> cide. The same thing is taking place right here." I literally saw the tanks
> going over people and crushing them. It was awful.

Self-Defense

Echoing throughout our interviews was the notion of "never again,"
which explains why it had been easy to find volunteers. Everyone was
willing to defend the nation. Furthermore, defying world opinion, Armenians of Nagorno-Karabakh did not stop with defending their own
towns and villages. When Azeris took much of the northern part of the
territory, Armenians did not hesitate to drive the Azeri population out
of strategic areas that made the Armenians vulnerable to attack. A politically sophisticated physician said, "Foreigners in general don't understand what is going on over here. What we are doing in Karabakh is
defending ourselves. We are conquering those areas where Azeris were
bombarding us, like Kelbajar or Agdam. Those were areas where Azeris
had strongholds bombarding us. All we have done is conquer those, taken
them away from them, simply to defend ourselves." In response to our
asking, "What is the military goal? How far will the military go?" she
replied, "Whatever it takes. We need to defend ourselves. Whatever area
is necessary to take away from the Azeris so that we can live peacefully."

People who had lost members of their family to the cause spoke of
their sacrifice almost matter-of-factly, as did a woman from Martakert
who said,

> For five years our village was at war. Our youth fought back. At the end
> of five years tanks entered our village. The enemy came with such force
> that all the young people tried to defend themselves. There were three hours
> of fighting, and they asked for help because they were overwhelmed. Some
> had to flee; some had to defend themselves. My son, Jalik, as he was defend-

ing himself and his village, was overtaken by a tank and killed. We
parents, wives, and children fled to the next village. We fled just the
way we were. There was rain, and many of us were without shoes.
It was raining.

Another woman and her husband evacuated their children by tractor to
Stepanakert, but her daughter told us that her mother said, "There is no
way that I can stay here in Stepanakert. I have to go back and be close
to my four sons, even though they are fighting." So this mother went
back and cooked for the soldiers defending their town. According to the
daughter, however, "The fighting got so bad that my brother thought it
best to take my mom out of there. He put her on the tractor, and they
were hiding behind trees, but the missile hit them anyway and my mom
was killed." When this same daughter was asked about people she knew
who had died because of the independence movement, she offered this
listing, starting with her father and her mother's sister and aunt, who
were in Baku:

> They came to their building, and they killed all of their seven children.
> So my aunt and her husband came to my mom's, to our village. There
> her husband was killed. Then my uncle's son died. He was killed. Another
> uncle's son was a dentist, and he was killed. His father, who was also a
> dentist, went to get his things, and they wouldn't let him; they killed him.
> My aunt was in Stepanakert in my mom's house, and a bomb fell, and she
> was all alone in the house, and she was killed.

Hence, another woman was probably not exaggerating when she said,
"When I went to Stepanakert the whole city had become a cemetery full
of dead Armenians—lives lost in the war." The same sentiment was
echoed by a man who said, "You know the brotherhood cemetery is full
now in Stepanakert. It is full of corpses, bodies of our youth. There is
no room to bury anyone anymore in that big cemetery, and it breaks my
heart." He continued his lament, saying, "Young men ages fifteen to early
twenties. It is just awful to realize that so many young people have given
up their lives. So many healthy, intelligent, young men." And in some
ways, it was not just the death of individuals; it was a blow to the collective body of Armenians, as was so eloquently stated by one person,
who said, "Every single soldier that dies is a heartache to us. It's our own
blood that's being shed. We feel with them. We sympathize with them.
It hurts us. Totally hurts us."

Equally painful, however, was the fact that many people who fell in combat could not be buried—or at least not buried properly. "I had my two-year-old grandchild on my back and was fleeing with my daughter-in-law. We eventually got to Stepanakert. This is where I heard about my son's death. I wanted to return to my village to bury him. I talked to soldiers, to people, to let me go, but they would not. They kept saying it wasn't safe. So my son was not buried." Another woman said, "I would like to see my husband just once. I would like to go back to my husband's grave. They buried him in such haste and left. I want to go and visit his grave. I wish we could go back."

Death, of course, was not the only result of the war. A nurse described the experience of working in a hospital: "We had hellish experiences in that we would see the wounded, the victims coming from the front on a daily basis. Boys, men who had lost arms and feet and hands and legs. It was just awful. Even injured children would come to the hospital." One of the most tragic cases was that of a young girl who had raised her hands to catch a ball and instead caught the force of an exploding shell. Her arms had to be amputated just below the elbows. Nevertheless, in the midst of this hellishness, people somehow found time for humor—perhaps to maintain their sanity.

> One day, it was September 10, a powerful, unbelievably wounded fellow came, and he was wrapped everywhere. Bandages on the legs, on the body, on the arms, on the head. His eyes were closed, and I thought what a pity, but I'm going to care for this fellow myself. Of course, all night long I stood by him and cared for him. I did anything I could. In the morning he opened his eyes, and when we asked him where he was, he said, "In Costa Rica." We knew that it was a joke, and we realized that in all that pain and all that awful condition, he could still joke with us. That was wonderful. This man was a refugee from Baku, and his attitude was, "If we don't defend Karabakh, who will?"

Voices from the War

Military history typically records what cities are taken on what dates and what destruction is done to industry supporting the war effort. But another way to tell the story is to attend to the voices of children and parents who lost their loved ones, as well as to the experiences and feelings of those fighting in the trenches. War takes its toll at many different levels. One woman told us, "I have lost all interest in life." As she was recounting a number of tragic events, she paused and said, "I've become emotionless. The way that I speak to you, I sound so callous." Her explanation for this blunting of emotion was this: "It's simply because I've been exposed to so many deaths that they have become common." And then she confessed, "I have wished that I were dead and my kids were dead. Life is so bitter."

> I lived with my husband for four years, and now I have to think about my children. I don't think about the future, actually. I think about today. I take one day at a time, worrying about how to feed them, how to clothe them, how to keep them clean. That's all I think of. I've lost all interest in life. Really, I've lost my beloved, I've lost my home, my country.

But in a moment of resolve, she said, "I will fight to the end," which seemed to be a common refrain and was encapsulated in the statement of a man who referred to the 1915 genocide and then said, "We are not dummies. We are not lambs ready for the slaughter." On the other hand, the positive drive, in contrast simply to the defensive action of staying alive, was the commitment to freedom. One man said, "I honor and respect independence," followed by the declaration, "I worship it!" This sentiment was echoed even by the children. A physician said about her daughter, "Oh yes. My daughter herself says, 'I want to grow up and go out there and fight and get our lands back.'"

Children Some of the most painful statements came from children whose fathers had been killed in the war. A boy of twelve said, "If I were to close my eyes and wish for something, I most of all would want my father. If I had my father, I would have everything. It is sad without him. My father would take me wherever I wanted to go. No one does that for me now." Another twelve-year-old said,

> I was close to my father. Now I don't have anyone to talk to. Sometimes I talk to my mother when I need to talk to someone. If I were to close my eyes and wish for something, it would certainly be my father. I wish that my father was alive, every day, especially when we sit down to eat. My mother has become very nice. She seldom gets upset at us. My sister and I try hard not to upset her.

Children whose fathers were still alive nevertheless lived with the constant fear that the war would take them away. For example, one six-year-old boy woke up crying, and when his mother asked him what was wrong, he said, "I dreamed about my dad. I dreamed about dad, and I know that he's not going to come home." A young mother whose husband was fighting said about her children, "Both of them miss their dad,

Children at the grave of their father near Yerevan.

very, very much. They remember the games that he played with them, the words that he spoke, the stories that he told them. They speak often about him." Her children were not alone in wishing for their dad's return: "You know, every so often cars come and bring soldiers back, fedayeen, the volunteer soldiers, and all the kids run to the car hoping to see their fathers. Some are very glad—they are joined by their fathers—but others are disappointed because just a few soldiers return at a time. The kids who do not see their fathers come home crying. It happened to our children."

Some children, of course, would never see their fathers return. A young adolescent described how he was told of his father's death:

> We plan to return to Karabakh in August. On August 8 it will be one year since my father died. He was fighting. We left Karabakh a month later, on September 8. I don't know exactly how my father died. From what I heard, he was with sixteen other friends when the Azeri Turks surrounded them and killed them all. The chief commander was the one who informed us. At that time my mother was in the hospital undergoing an operation. The commander told my uncle first, then my uncle told me and my sister that my father was wounded. When we went to the hospital, on the way to

the hospital, they told me that my father had died. Our lives have become difficult in every way since my father's death.

When this twelve-year-old finished saying this, he started crying.

Women and Parents   Although women who lost their husbands in the war were paid small pensions, life was very difficult for many of them. Many of these women and their children were virtually homeless. A woman living in Yerevan with her daughters said, "No, I don't work now. I was willing to do anything, but I haven't found anything yet. See, we are refugees." She then explained what happened. "It was June when the Turks entered our village, and my husband was killed as he was defending us. So we fled to Stepanakert. We only stayed there for a few days because there was nowhere for us to stay and it too was being bombarded." From there they went to Armenia. "For a couple of months we stayed with some relatives in Yerevan. For the last nine or ten months we have been here in Arzni, in this hotel, a place for people [who are homeless because of the war] to stay."

Because of the fear of becoming a widow, not every wife supported her husband's decision to go to war. One woman said, "Of course I was against it. I didn't want him to go. I was alone and I had this baby, and how in the world was I going to get food for her? How could I do without him? But he made a decision, and for him it was more important to go to the front with all these men." Some women recognized that the war was not just difficult for the Armenians; it was equally traumatic for the wives of the enemy. A woman who had lost her husband in the war said, "I have two orphans, and I don't want my enemies to have orphans. As much as they are enemies I don't want them to have orphans. It's a terrible thing to have orphans." In her view, the war was senseless, even though she said that Nagorno-Karabakh is a holy land. The family, she said, is also holy, and the war is ripping families apart.

Worrying about husbands and sons who were missing in action was, in some ways, as stressful as the knowledge that they had been killed. A father said that his son disappeared somewhere in the Martakert region. "I still don't know if he is dead or alive. I asked a lot of people about him, but they were only able to describe how well he fought for those places." This father went to the village where he was last seen and showed people his son's picture. Apparently the commander of the battalion told him that he had ordered his men back into combat, to "bring my son, Avet, back, dead or alive." Avet's father even went to the morgue to look for his son's body, but without success. In the interview he lamented that

Grandfather with infant. Yerevan.

Psychiatrist who spent two years working with survivors after 1988 earthquake.
Yerevan.

Three generations confronting consequences of 1988 earthquake. Nalband, near Spitak.

Earthquake damaged church, Gyumri

Children playing near ruins
of their school. Spitak.

Girl playing in earthquake rubble. Spitak.

Earthquake victim. Spitak.

Woman who survived both the 1915 genocide and 1988 earthquake. Spitak

Man taking a break while reconstructing his own house. Gyumri.

Funeral procession; cars bear images of those lost. Gyumri.

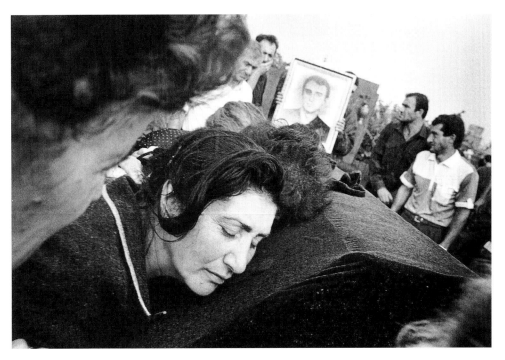

Mourner in a funeral procession. Gyumri.

Solemn crowd in a funeral procession. Gyumri.

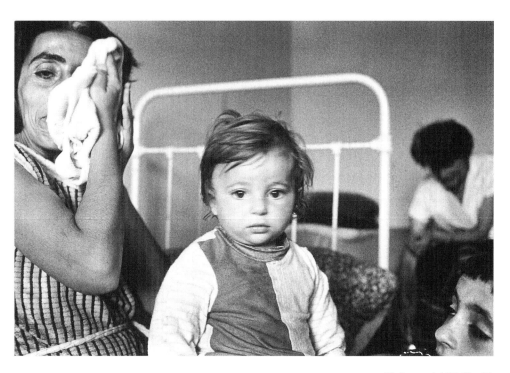

Mother and child. Shushi.

Daily life on the streets. Stepanakert.

Armenian families reclaiming the streets of Shushi.

Children playing. Shushi.

Women waiting for helicopters at military hospital to discover if husbands or sons are among dead or wounded. Stepanakert.

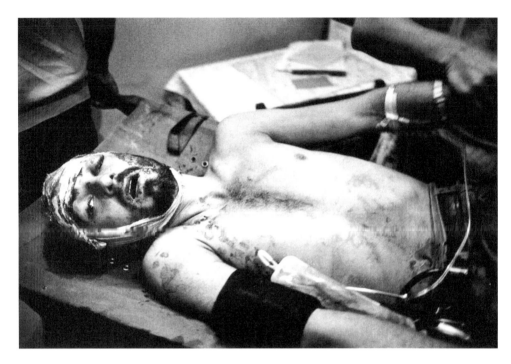

Wounded soldier awaiting treatment in military hospital. Stepanakert.

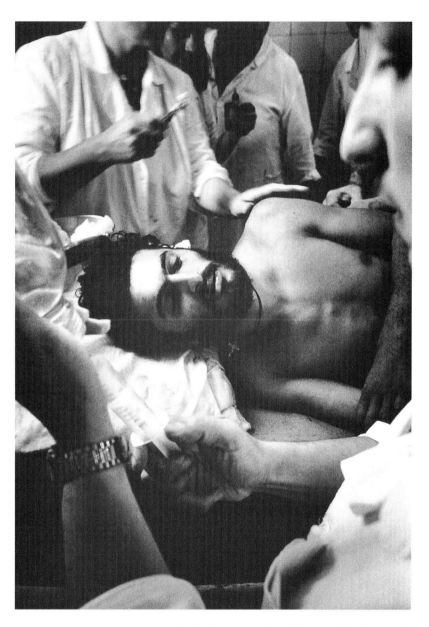

Wounded soldier being treated in military hospital. Stepanakert.

Wounded civilian at military hospital. Stepanakert.

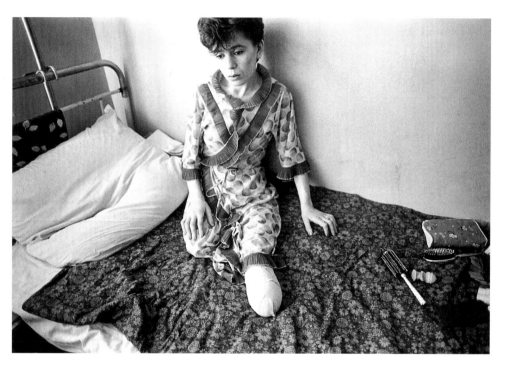
Mother injured by land mine in Nagorno-Karabakh. Yerevan.

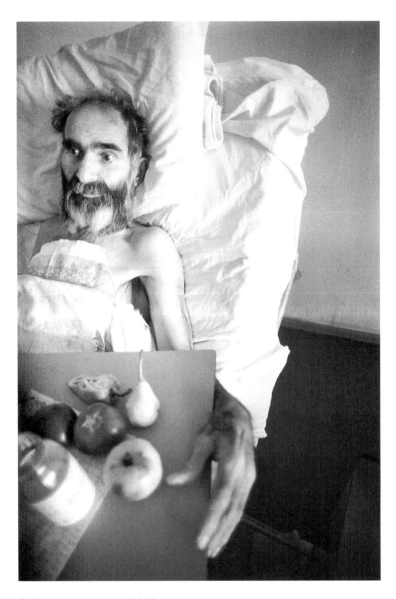

Soldier recovering in hospital. Yerevan.

Soldier in cemetery. Yerevan.

Battalion leader in cemetery near Yerevan where some of his young soldiers are buried.

Man praying. Yerevan.

A tightrope walker. Yerevan.

Waiting for kerosene during winter. Yerevan.

Bread distribution. Yerevan.

Family attempting to stay warm in kitchen during winter. Yerevan.

Selling personal and household items in flea market. Yerevan.

Child studying in primary school. Yerevan.

Celebrating marriage during snowstorm. Yerevan.

Advertising items for sale during winter. Yerevan.

Public transportation. Yerevan.

Bodies of soldiers brought to Yerevan from Nagorno-Karabakh.

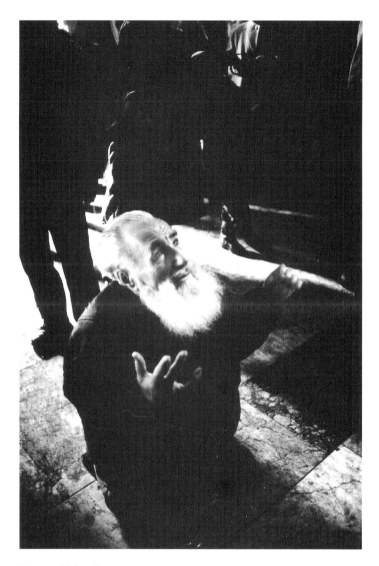

Man worshiping. Yerevan.

Public transportation. Yerevan.

Boy praying in church. Shushi.

Girl in doorway of reoccupied house. Shushi.

Leaving Armenia, winter 1994. Yerevan.

in nine days his son would be twenty-one. A woman said about her sons, "I worry a lot about my boys. I don't know where they are. I don't know how they are. I cry often."

On the other hand, soldiers were often able to communicate with their loved ones. A young mother said that one day some soldiers brought her a letter from her husband.

> It really uplifted me. It was such a beautiful, beautiful letter, and I read it to my friends as well. He [her husband] had sent milk for my baby. I read the letter to my friends whose husbands were also in the war. It was a wonderful letter. It uplifted all of us. It strengthened us. It gave us hope. He didn't use big words, but the words came from his heart. It gave us a wonderful message, comforting us, showing us that we, too, were in the same situation—that we all needed each other.

Unfortunately, her husband was later killed.

A group of female university students said that the men had disappeared from the city. "When we walk on the streets we do not see any young, healthy fellows anymore. The only fellows that we see are the ones who have been handicapped or crippled by the war." And, indeed, that was the plight of many women, to care for their wounded husbands and sons. In a few cases the wounded were sent out of the country for medical treatment, such as one soldier who went to France, but more often the injured were treated in the local medical facilities. One woman mentioned that her husband had been wounded and was now at home: "He cannot do much. He can't work, only very light kinds of jobs. He could be a guard, or something like that. He feels very nervous because he's idle and he wants to work, but right now there is nothing."

Soldiers   By focusing on the plight of women and children, we do not mean to minimize the anguish experienced on the front lines. Particularly in the early days of the conflict, it was a David and Goliath struggle. The Azeris had the tanks and the support of the Russians, and the Armenians were trying to stop their assault with rifles, which had about the same effect as a slingshot might have against plated armor. Later on, however, the Armenians acquired more sophisticated armaments, in part because they confiscated weapons from the Azeris. One soldier told us that in Martakert they captured forty-seven tanks. And like David of old, those with heart often overcame those who were merely fighting out of obligation. Our interviewees often implied that the war was a spiritual battle: They were fighting for their souls—for their land.

One soldier said, "You're reconciled with death." He viewed his life as being in a lottery where there was a chance, maybe even a good possibility, that he would be killed. On the other hand, the purpose was clear, and once the war started there was no backing down. Armenians were fighting for their very survival, a point that was amply demonstrated in the Sumgait massacres and in the treatment of noncombatants in the war zone. We must also note that men were not the only soldiers. As one man told us, "From Martakert we had a woman, her name was Haygoush, she was forty-five years old. She told us that the Turks had killed her husband and so she wanted to fight. So we let her." This same person said that he knew another female soldier who killed one of the enemy and then said, "It served him right. I only gunned him down. He should have been skinned instead." This interviewee said that he admired the courage of the women soldiers. "They fight well. They fight like men." Apparently the women, at least according to one soldier, were called "sisters." He said there were women from Armenia, Nagorno-Karabakh, and Sumgait, and that the Sumgait women, in particular, were there to avenge the deaths of their husbands.

Although not all Armenian soldiers treated their enemies well, it is important to note that some of the soldiers said they observed an honor code in battle. Specifically, one soldier said, "We do not touch the women of our enemy. We respect them. We stay Armenian; we stay Christian." This same person said, "In war there is nothing good. Nothing good exists in war. We all want peace. We fighters want peace. Our enemy fighters want peace." For every soldier killed, there is a family that is also injured, hurt. This point was poignantly made by a woman who spoke of the killing of an eighteen-year-old boy. Referring to the father, she said, "His father—he was such a neat fellow—died seven months after that [the death of the son] from a broken heart."

The fathers who were in the war spoke of how much they missed their children while they were away. One soldier said, "I have three children—six, five, and three. I don't think my three-year-old child knows me. When the older ones call me 'Dad,' he follows suit, but that's about it. It is hard, but then I have to think about our goal. I am out here protecting them, defending them. I want them to be happy, so it's okay if the young one does not recognize me. It's not a big issue. We have to have patience, and we have to look forward to victory." Another soldier similarly connected the purpose of the war to his children. "We are fighting for our freedom. We are fighting for the freedom of all Armenians. Yes, it has been long, but our families are at stake. Their safety, their lives are at stake. We need

Grave in Stepanakert. Women sometimes fought alongside men on the front lines.

to protect them to the end, to the last soldier." And a man who had been wounded in the war said, "Our kids deserve peace," arguing that the war was only justifiable because of the savage attacks that had been initiated by the Azeris against the Armenians.

Refugee Status in Armenia

Thousands of Armenian refugees were created when the Azeris took the Martakert region and other areas. Once the available housing was filled in Stepanakert, Armenia was one of the logical places for people to re-settle. In spite of the fact that the fledgling Republic of Armenia was strug-gling for its own survival, refugees from Nagorno-Karabakh were ac-commodated there as well. One woman said, "We received a real welcome from Armenia. I feel very grateful. Ever since we have been here, we have received clothing and food. People have been good to us. We have also received help from overseas. I don't know what we would have done without this help. I will be grateful until the end of my life." An-other refugee voiced almost identical feelings. "Oh, we were well received. They gave us this place to stay, and they gave us clothing and food. They helped us to settle down here in Armenia."

The conduit of some of this aid was the Artsakh Committee in Ar-menia. In addition to settling refugees from Nagorno-Karabakh in ho-tels, sanatoriums, and other available housing, the committee gave finan-cial aid to people who had a family member killed or injured. One woman whose husband died said, "They give a sum of a hundred thousand rubles to the family that loses a victim and twelve thousand monthly if there are children." A woman whose husband was wounded stated, "The Art-sakh Committee gives us fifteen hundred rubles a month; they give us three kilos of beans, butter, and powered milk. They give us that because we have a wounded member in the family."

Some families that resettled in Armenia received food aid from rela-tives who remained in Nagorno-Karabakh. A young woman with chil-dren said, "We could get things from Karabakh like flour and vegeta-bles. Our relatives sent them to us, so we were just barely surviving." Others indicated that their friends in Nagorno-Karabakh were much bet-ter off than they were in Armenia because it was easier to keep livestock and chickens in Nagorno-Karabakh. The blockade meant that refugees faced the same difficulties as did the rest of the population of Armenia. They struggled to stay warm, they were often without electricity, and food was scarce. A woman with several children said that, initially, she stayed with her brothers in Armenia, but she didn't want to impose on them too long. Furthermore, she said, "We didn't have enough warm clothes. We were here December 1992. There was no bread, no money. We had no documents. It was very miserable." Also, her brother, who was a doctor, had his car stolen in Armenia. She said, "It was awful. Under my care I had five kids. One of them was hurt in the war, and here I had to care for them, when food prices were high; when it was extremely cold; when I could only get potatoes, macaroni, and rice; when

I could see my own breath. It was that cold, and it felt like we were in Siberia."

On the other hand, there were moments of relief. An Armenian organization from Iran took a number of orphan children over six years of age for a period of three months. "They came back with new clothes, jewelry; it was wonderful." Volunteers from the United States set up special programs, such as the one established by a woman from Los Angeles for children who were not in school. "She always comes and teaches my children songs and things like that. It makes me feel so good that she takes her time to do that. It comforts us." The sponsorship programs, food, and money sent to refugees by people from overseas provided significant relief. A mother said, "There are some people in America. They are sponsoring, and we are thankful. They send money from time to time. If it weren't for those people's help, we couldn't survive."

At the same time, there was an enormous sense of goodwill among refugees, who tried to help each other in times of difficulty. A soldier said, "All neighbors support one another. You don't have to be related to love the other. You are just neighbors, and that is enough." He continued, "They support one another, stand together against the enemy." A woman acknowledged the difficulty of surviving but then pointed to the support of friends. "We had a shortage of food and we were only given one kilogram, that is, two pounds, of flour. How could I feed a family of five with one kilogram of flour? It was impossible. You know, under these difficult circumstances people were helping one another, giving each other whatever they could not use, so that nobody would go without food." One woman described how they communicated their needs in a thirteen-story sanatorium where refugees had been placed. They would call from one balcony to another, sharing food, informing each other of who had died in the war and who was sick. She concluded by saying, "So those were sad days, really sad days, where things were difficult to bear." The overriding point, however, is that refugees supported one another in a heroic fashion. They were bound together by their losses. They knew that their salvation rested in assisting and supporting one another.

Ending the War

Everyone we interviewed anticipated the day when the war would be over and things could return to normal. The phrase "return to normal" meant many different things. For refugees, it meant returning home. For others, it meant cessation of the blockade and the possibility of the economy reviving. For everyone, it meant adequate supplies of energy for light, transportation, heat during the winter months, and plentiful food.

We encountered almost no one who said that the war was wrong. But we did interview people who said that they never anticipated the consequences of supporting Nagorno-Karabakh's independence. For example, a man who was active in the demonstrations said, "It looked like it was going to be something simple. I never realized that it was going to get us into this big war." The ecstasy associated with the demonstrations had paled by the time of our interviews. No one had contemplated the reality of loved ones dying and of living a life of blockade-induced physical deprivation. On the other hand, many people compared their situation to what confronted Armenians in 1915. Then very few Armenians resisted. They were slaughtered like sheep and died agonizing deaths from starvation, dehydration, and deportation-related diseases, such as typhoid. That mistake was too strong in the collective memory to be repeated. One man said that he was reconciled to the fact that his son was a sergeant in the army and ran the risk of being killed. He said, "When you look at 1915, when we were killed, when the genocide took place, when the Turks killed us by the millions, it was much, much worse than what we are facing today." In his view, "If we do lose, we have no right to exist." In fact, his desire was not only to liberate Nagorno-Karabakh, but to get back all of their historic lands. "Turks, Azeris, Georgians, Persians—they all owe us our land. I would like to see it all returned."

But the cost of war was extremely high on both sides. Many people recognized that it was not just Armenian lives that were being lost, but also Azeri lives. One woman pessimistically said that she thought the war would probably continue, but also felt that it had gone on long enough. "It has lasted six years now. So many homes are broken because there is no male there: husbands have died, sons have died, fathers have died." She said that her sixteen-year-old cousin had died, and when he entered the army his mother was all for his involvement. "She said, 'You go and defend our country,' and she inspired the son to go, and he went and died in the war. [But] now she is insane. Mentally she has lost it from grief." Another person graphically stated, "We have to get over this Karabakh thing. It's been too long. The knife now has cut to the bone." A female physician commented, "I don't think our people realized how long it was going to go on. Time and again it has stopped and started, stopped and started again." In her opinion, "The common people, the average person, will be so thankful once there is peace and quiet. The Azeris will be happy. The Armenians will be happy. We'll all go back to our normal lives." She then stated emphatically, "We need to go forward. We can't go back. We need to go forward."

Many people said that a political compromise between the two sides should be negotiated. A man in his seventies said, "Both sides need to get together and sign a peace contract and end the war. We need peace and harmony. The war doesn't help us, and it doesn't help them either." If the two parties could simply get together, both sides would compromise, said a young woman. "Everyone is already sick and tired of the war. People want peace." A woman who grew up in a politically sophisticated home said, "They have to come to the point where there is equality between the countries. The answer is not in destroying one another, competing as to who sheds more blood. We can attack Baku; they can attack Stepanakert. Armenians have to defend Stepanakert; Azeris have to defend Baku. It is sad to see that all we have right now is bloodshed." The middle ground, argued another person, is that these two countries have coexisted in the past, and they must learn to do it once again. "It is possible to have compromise between Azeris and Armenians. After all, they have been neighbors, and they have lived together for many years. They can have things in common. They can come to an agreement. There can be peace if people do not oppose it." In some ways, the basis for peace is that neither side is winning. "Both sides are losing," said one individual. Citing the futility of the current conflict, a female physician said, "It is not a war of land; it's a war of bloodshed. You killed my father; I'm going to kill your father. You killed my cousin; I'm going to kill you. So it is, back and forth, a revenge type of thing. You go and kill because they killed your own. They kill because you killed them. You kill them because they kill you." Even though this person did not think the war was over territory, people were obviously gaining and losing land as a result of these hard-fought battles. Either Nagorno-Karabakh will be independent, or it will return to being ruled by the Azeris. The only sense in which *both* sides are losing is that soldiers are being killed and maimed on both sides. But territory is being gained or lost in those battles, and military advantage is being gained by one side and not the other. One person compared the war to the war in Vietnam. The American engagement in Vietnam was protracted, and it seemed as if the war would never end. But eventually the Americans left, he said. And that was his hope regarding the Azeris—that they would grow tired of the conflict and simply decide to allow Nagorno-Karabakh to be independent.

Many people saw Russia as holding the key to the achievement of peace. At one level, Russia was to blame for creating the problem in the first place. A scientist minced few words in setting the context for the conflict. "It was that scum, idiot Stalin. Usually one fool makes a mistake, and a hundred smart people have to correct it. He took a part of Armenia and gave it to Azerbaijan, and now so many people are dying while trying to correct his foolish mistake. Now redefining the borders is as painful as cutting someone's flesh when that person is alive." But some people also recognized that Nagorno-Karabakh's salvation also rests with Russia. "If Russia were not here, we would have been conquered by the Azeris a long time ago. But because of Russia, we've survived." On the other hand, some people felt that Russia's real self-interest was in perpetuating the war, thereby keeping each side weak and under its thumb. With regard to the United States, even though it was providing humanitarian aid, no one thought that the United States had the power to settle the conflict. And Turkey was recognized as being strictly on the Azeri side. One person stated his view emphatically: "How can Turkey be a peacemaker when it directly participates in Armenia's blockade? Turkey supports Azerbaijan in any way possible and represents, in the United Nations, Azerbaijan's interests. It is not neutral. Therefore, Turkey has no moral right to be a mediator in this conflict. Russia could be."

At one level, Armenians felt helpless to end the conflict. At best, they hoped to create a position of advantage, so that if peace talks were to occur, they could at least negotiate from a position of strength. One person somewhat fatalistically said that there had to be an international desire to end the conflict. "It's not up to us. Other nations have to step in. If they say yes, it will end." The bottom line of all negotiation, said interviewees, is independence for Nagorno-Karabakh. Too much blood had been shed by the Armenians to return to the previous arrangement—even if it were to be an independent enclave under the Republic of Azerbaijan. People who had sacrificed their sons and husbands in the war were not inclined toward a cheap compromise, because that would completely invalidate the price they had already paid. The following feeling was widely present in the Armenian community:

> I always think about my son. How can I not think about my son? I am a mother, you know. But when you see injustice, when you see torture, when you see such vicious enemies, you just get so angry that nothing seems too hard to do. I would go to the front if need be. I would care for the wounded,

and I would kill a Turk. I wouldn't give a damn if they killed me. That's how I feel. I really do.

Contrary to the assumption of some people in the international community, our interviews revealed little desire for Nagorno-Karabakh to be under the rule of the Republic of Armenia. Rather, the prevailing sentiment was that it should be an independent country. Obviously, it would have strong ties to Armenia, but it would also have its own governance structure. There was widespread recognition that Nagorno-Karabakh people are different, and the land itself is unique. Sharing his own experience, a refugee from Baku said, "Karabakh is a very noble land, and the Karabakh people are very hardworking. I know that, because I have been there often. When I was waking up there at four or five in the morning, they were already working." Thus many of the people we interviewed had a strong faith that Nagorno-Karabakh would prevail. Not only did they feel that they had the moral high ground, but they had the tenacity, courage, and fortitude to win the war, almost regardless of the costs involved.

Many volunteers from Armenia shared this view. A young man from the earthquake region in Armenia told how his commitment was sealed:

> When the first victim came, that's when I got really stirred up. I had this powerful patriotic feeling within me for justice. This happened two years ago, and I was full of vengeance. This young, beautiful childhood friend of mine, healthy, went and sacrificed himself in the battle for Shushi. That's when I decided that I would have to take his place and take my revenge.
>
> When Turks entered Martakert and other villages, people were helpless. Now we have all the arms we need. We got them from the Turks by fear and by deception. We have tanks, and we have guns, and we are well armed. They respect us for this. We call ourselves "Free Citizens of Karabakh." Everywhere we go we are welcomed. They respect us. They thank us. They know that we are saving their lives. We work together with Karabakh soldiers. They have been fighting for five years, and I myself for two years. They are dedicated and they welcome us, knowing we are from Leninakan. They welcome us and are proud of us.

He explained that they were an independent group that had gone voluntarily to the front. They were not drafted or coerced by the government of the Republic of Armenia. He said that when they went back to their own city in Armenia, the Nagorno-Karabakh soldiers would cry. "The Karabakh soldiers feel good that we fight right along with them. You see, we give them moral support. Side by side we fight."

In addition, Armenians from overseas came to fight. Referring to the

Dashnak political party, a resident of Stepanakert said, "They have helped us in the past, and they are helping us now." She said that the Hnchak party members were also assisting them. In fact, one of the key strategists for the war effort was a young Armenian from Visalia, California, who was later killed in the war. Explaining the unity of Armenians around the issue of Nagorno-Karabakh's independence, a soldier from Nagorno-Karabakh stated: "An Armenian is an Armenian, whether in Karabakh or Armenia," and he probably should have added, whether in Pasadena, São Paulo, or Beirut.

The Future

When Armenians talk about Nagorno-Karabakh, they often have a sense of reverence in their voice. The land is sacred. It appears to parallel the Promised Land of the people of Israel. A woman who fled her village during the war reminisced, "The Karabakh land, the land is gold. It's a gold mine there. It's very rich soil, very fruitful and productive." People who left during the war said that they would inevitably return, even if their homes had been destroyed. When asked if she would return with her children, even if their house had been burned and their farm land ruined, this mother replied, "We can always start from scratch and build it up again." "After all," she said, "it is our village, and we can live there. We will return, and we will start building again. We are not afraid of work." Another refugee from Nagorno-Karabakh stated almost the same thing, but more poetically.

> There is a song in Armenian where the swallow sings that she is building her nest. Every time she adds a new branch, she thinks of her old nest. That's how I feel. I feel like our old nest is ruined and we're building a new nest. But as we try to build a new nest we cannot forget the old nest. We always remember our old nest. Just like the swallow, we want to go back to our old home.

And a woman whose son was killed in the war said, "You know, I prefer dry bread in my village than anywhere else with good food. If we go back, and I hope we will, we can rebuild. We can get back our soil and harvest it and till it and plant things and we can live, if we go back."

This same love of the land and sense of place were expressed by a woman who lost her husband during the war. "I would go today, and I would go running to my village. I know that my house was burned, but that would not stop me. I would go running, and I would start building, and I would take my family back. That is where we belong." This woman speaks for all Armenians, including those in the diaspora, when she says, "Armenians are creative people, and no matter how many times you knock them down, they get back up again. You destroy their homes and village, and they get up again and build again. So that is what we will do."

4

Surviving the Winter

Paying the Price for Independence

We clearly remember flying into the Yerevan airport in May of 1993. Except for several lights on the runway, the capital city of the Republic of Armenia was dark. There were no streetlights. Not a single house was illuminated by an electric light bulb. We didn't even see the headlights of automobiles. From the air, Yerevan looked like it must have appeared in the Middle Ages.

By the time we finally collected our baggage and checked through customs, the sun was illuminating the city. Since we had American dollars, it was relatively easy to get a cab to take us to the Hotel Armenia. But on the way we noticed a sight we didn't want to see. Many of the limbs on trees had been cut back by people desperate for firewood, and now the spring foliage was hugging the naked trunks. We feared that the forests of Armenia had suffered similar depredation. We also saw people piling out of a streetcar and filing up the road. The electricity in the overhead grid had stopped, and people were heading to their destinations on foot. When we arrived at the hotel lobby, the lights were on, but as we checked into our favorite room on the fifth floor we heard a generator roaring in the background. The floor maid told us that we should draw a full tub when the water came on, because otherwise we would not be able to bathe in the morning. That was fair warning, and fortunately we had brought our camping shower—a black plastic bag with a nozzle that we hung out on the porch to warm.

Compared with most residents of the city, we were in luxurious surroundings. For the first two weeks of January, many homes had no electricity, and this was in a city filled with high-rise apartments. Not only was there no heat in the dead of winter, but people often had to carry water up many flights of stairs. Furthermore, food was severely rationed. The official quota was 250 grams of bread a day per person. Unemployment was 80 percent in many districts, and people had long ago run out of savings because of hyperinflation. Monthly pensions that might have been comfortable only a few years earlier would scarcely buy a few weeks' worth of bread. People were selling household items at a fraction of their worth, and consequently the open-air flea market was one of the only thriving commercial enterprises. Laid out for display were silverware, dishes, used rugs, embroidered tablecloths, clothing, and various tools. Many people had already sold wedding rings, jewelry, and other personal items. More people were selling than buying, because very few people had any discretionary income.

When we first visited Armenia in 1990, the capital city was alive with activity. Everywhere around the hotel there were fountains. The theaters were full. Children were riding a miniature roller coaster in the park. When we tried to buy an ice cream cone, we made very little forward progress as people crowded in ahead of us—everyone seemed to have loose change to spare. And the women were dressed elegantly, sporting European fashions. Hence, it was with sinking hearts that we stepped outside the hotel three years later. The construction crane rising from a half-finished basement in the lot next door was rusting. There was no water in the fountains. People were walking in the park, but weeds were growing up around the idle roller coaster. From the appearance of the street lights, someone had been pirating the copper wire to sell abroad. Later we heard that whole factories were being dismantled, often for the value of the steel alone.

A few days later we had dinner with a noted scientist. He was generating electricity from a miniature windmill that he had rigged up on his tenth-story balcony. The current fed into several car batteries, which lighted twelve-volt bulbs that were hanging from the chandelier in the dining room. We were served fish from Lake Sevan, which we knew was an extravagant expression of affection for Lorna's brother-in-law, who was a fellow physicist and had been generous in lecturing at the Polytechnic Institute. We walked home in the dark that night, glad that we had brought flashlights, which clearly marked us as outsiders, since everyone else went unaided, not able to afford the luxury of batteries. The next day we hired a cab to take us around the city and we could not figure out why the driver kept turning off the ignition. Later we realized that he was saving fuel on the downhill portions of the trip.

The first time we came to Yerevan in 1990, we brought American cigarettes—Marlboros, to be exact. This time, we brought a Polaroid camera. But we soon learned that giving away pictures of kids could cause a near riot, because many of the children had not had a photo taken in several years. What really broke our hearts, however, was going into the markets. Typically, there were only a few cans on the shelves and a rancid-looking piece of meat or cheese behind the counter. Not only did people have no money to spend, but there was nothing to buy.

Food

Many people told us that they lost between twenty and thirty pounds during the winters of 1993 and 1994. Our experience of Armenians, especially the older generation, is that they are rotund. Grandmothers pinch the cheeks of children and scold the parents if a child is too thin. But now the clothes hung on people we interviewed. The typical diet was a piece of bread, and sometimes macaroni, potatoes, or rice. Butter was a luxury item, and meat was nearly unheard of, except on special occasions when a momentous birthday or some other event was celebrated. Because electricity was extremely intermittent, often coming on for only an hour or two, if that, much of the food was eaten cold. When there was power, mothers fixed soup and prepared food for the next day.

People living in rural areas tended to fare better than those in the cities. They could live off the land, whereas those in the city had become used to exchanging money for food. After the first cold winter, people wanted to make preserves of fruit and other goods for the winter, but they seldom had money to buy the raw materials. Sometimes relatives living on farms would come to their rescue. Occasionally someone would get a small gift from a relative living in the United States or Europe. One woman said, "My husband's uncle who lives in France was very generous. He is a hard-working man, and he bought me a fur coat and gave us a hundred dollars. We really appreciated it. It was so wonderful of him. We know that he's a hard-working man. He's not a rich man, and yet he wants to share." And a few people received aid from international organizations, typically consisting of rice, beans and/or wheat, powdered milk, oil, butter, vermicelli, and sometimes canned meat. Coffee, a perennial favorite of Armenians, was almost absent from their diets. Instead, tea was substituted because it was cheaper. Sugar was used very sparingly, if at all. In some areas, potatoes seemed relatively easy to get, and one person told us that her family alternated between eating rice one night and potatoes the next.

One of our interviewers was scolded in a joking manner because she mentioned the word "meat" in a question. This man said that his young children didn't know what the word meant—they had never eaten meat. Many people said that the dominant conversation among friends and family members revolved around food: the good old days when it was plentiful; the present problem of food—how much it cost and where it could be found; and the way that the scarcity was affecting the young. A retired elementary school teacher said, "All we can afford is potatoes and pasta. Even animals need variety in their diet. Isn't it a shame that we only talk about bread, and we don't even talk about wonderful things like culture?" Another elderly woman reported her grandchild asking her, "Grandma, isn't eggplant growing anymore?" She said, "They don't know that it does grow, just that grandma does not have enough money to buy it." Instead, she made apricot jam for the children, skimping, she said, on the sugar.

The more poignant stories were of children crying themselves to sleep or mothers putting their kids to bed at six o'clock in the evening so that they would not feel the pangs of hunger so much. Several people witnessed the following scene, and the story was circulating:

> This little girl apparently didn't have bread, and she was asking people to give her bread, and a guy felt sorry for her and said to the people who were in the area, "Why don't you each give something to this poor kid. After all, she's hungry." So everyone gave a little bit of money, and she got quite a bit and she was so happy. She gathered all the money and ran home to give the good news to her mother. When she got home her mother had committed suicide. She was hanging from a rope.

Armenians were shocked to see people begging, a practice unheard of until after independence. In particular, one person we interviewed was pained by the fact that elderly people who had worked all their lives and led a dignified existence were now forced to hold out their hands to

Stockpiling food for winter in Yerevan.

strangers. Another individual told us about an eight-year-old boy who was singing in a darkened subway station, hoping that people would put a few coins in his hand. For this independent and self-sufficient people, such acts of humiliation were nearly unthinkable. People were also humiliated by their inability to keep the time-honored custom of offering guests a cup of coffee and a pastry. They were lucky to have their share of 250 grams of bread. A woman who had lost her daughter in the earthquake said, "We have suffered long enough. Now all we think about when we wake up in the morning is bread. How am I going to get bread? That's all we think about. That's what we have come down to. It's sad, you know." The preoccupation with food clearly sapped the spirit of the people. "I love culture," said an unemployed woman engineer. "I always enjoyed books and the theater. I've forgotten all that. Culture is gone. There is no growth, psychologically or spiritually. All we think about is food. How can we feed our children? That is all our minds are occupied with."

For those living on pensions, even subsistence survival was difficult. A man in his sixties stated that he received 143 drams a month. "With 143 I can get a half kilogram of meat, or I can get fifteen eggs, or I can get a half kilogram of butter." Instead, he bought potatoes, because he

Until recently, begging was uncommon; now it is sometimes the only means of survival for the elderly, such as this man from Yerevan.

could buy 15–20 kilograms with his monthly salary. Such trade-offs were not part of life under the communists—at least in recent years.

Foreign assistance did reach some people, although it was uneven and irregular. For example, a woman said, "Shoghik [her daughter] takes piano lessons, and so her conservatory gave her powdered milk, raisins, flour, and cracked wheat. She was so happy and so enthused about this whole thing. She thought it was her reward for performing well. Anyway, we profited from it, of course, as a family." And a policeman said that his wife nursed their newborn son for six months and now the child was receiving powdered milk from the Red Cross, the result of funding from the United States, Germany, and France. Various religious organizations, such as the Armenian Missionary Association of America (AMAA) gave aid to selected needy families. People told us that they were very grateful for the monthly rations of macaroni, rice, flour, butter, and oil that their families received. An elderly man said they had received assistance before, citing the Armenian General Benevolent Union (AGBU):

> I experienced another famine, that was after the 1915 genocide. I remember in Yerevan there was total starvation. People would sleep on the streets and not wake up in the morning. The death toll was high, and the United States

came to our aid. Charity organizations like AGBU and others brought food to us to help us, to save us from starvation. I even remember a building right behind the church, Holy Sarkis, where they had a restaurant, and they fed us. I remember I would go with my mother and would have such delicious food. The Americans did that; we were so thankful. Even today it is the American charity organizations that have helped us.

Referring to the present time of hardship, he said, "We have received flour, oil, beans, preserves, and we are thankful, thankful, thankful! If it weren't for them [AGBU], this would be another starvation time for us. Many thanks to these charity organizations." On the other hand, aid was clearly not available to everyone. When we asked one woman whether she had received aid during the winter, she said simply, "We did not know where to apply for it."

Bread Lines

One of the traumas of food shortage in the country was that people were given coupons to redeem in bread distribution centers, but these centers were not well stocked, and bread delivery was highly irregular—in part because energy supplies were so erratic, but also because of government inefficiency, said many people. The frustration was that people would sometimes wait for hours and then be turned away because the supply of bread had run out, or the time for distribution had elapsed, or they were saving bread to distribute the following day. One man said, "I've waited so many nights. Two to three times a month, after waiting all night long, there will be no bread, and they always have an excuse, saying there was no flour, or transportation was down, or whatever." Because of the shortage, people would queue for hours before the distribution sites opened. A woman said that she and her husband would go at 2 A.M. and wait until 6 A.M. to get their bread. As a survival technique, apparently, sometimes people would stand all those hours without even talking to one another; when they did speak, fights would break out.

> There were no lights in houses, and we stood in lines in complete darkness. Before the car with bread arrived, people knew who was after whom in the line. But once the distribution of bread began, people just attacked it. They were too tired and too frustrated after waiting for such a long time. Often, some people, after buying bread, fell on the ground on their way out of line. And often we would get nothing and returned home empty handed. Sometimes we stood in line from 7 P.M. to 4 A.M. and returned home with nothing.

Waiting in line for bread in Yerevan.

Sometimes there appeared to be corruption or collusion regarding who received bread.

> Everyone was given a number, and I was given number 13. So I was in front of the bakery at 7 A.M. and all day long. At 7 P.M. I was still standing there, and I had no bread yet. Two trucks came and delivered their bread. Time and again, strong gangster-type guys would come by, cut into the lines, and get the bread. It almost seemed like distributors were siding with them. It was 7 P.M. and the doors closed, and they told us that was all.

In desperation, this seventy-eight-year-old man took matters into his own hands:

> Here I was, number 13, and no bread. I got so angry. I was beside myself with anger. I shouted and said, "Open the door. We need bread!" They said, "No, this is all for today," and I shouted again and I said, "If you do not open the door and give me bread, I'm going to break the window." They didn't seem to believe me. Well, I was so angry then, I can't believe it myself now as I'm talking, but I was so angry and so upset that I went back and got a big rock and I threw it with all the force I had at the window of the door, and it shattered to pieces.

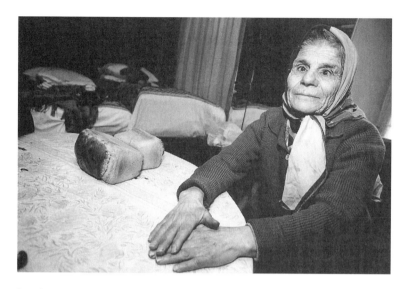

Bread was the primary source of nutrition for many Armenians. This woman lives in Yerevan.

In response, the people distributing the bread came looking for the culprit, and the crowd pointed at him and he said, "If you don't give me bread, this is what I do." So they took him inside, and he thought they were going to kill him. Instead, he lectured them. "I told them how unfair they had been all day, and I said, 'I'm a teacher. I've been a teacher for many years, and look what you've made me do.' They kept me there all night, and they left. I didn't care. I picked up some bread and ate it. With such gusto, right in front of them, like an animal, just to show them my anger."

A woman said that she also witnessed "ruffians" (her term) crowding into bread lines. "It used to be so ugly. They used to push to the front and get the bread, and here we had been waiting all along and didn't get anything. The bread would all be gone. Then we'd have to wait for the next truck to arrive." In response, she said that once she also started shoving. The person in charge rebuked her, saying, "How selfish of you to get in here!" Unlike the elderly gentleman who took his revenge, she gave up. "I felt it was so unfair. So instead of talking back to him, I just cried. I thought, 'How awful. How humiliating this has become.'"

Economics

The salaries of people who were fortunate enough to be employed averaged 3,000–5,000 rubles a month among those whom we interviewed, although several people reported salaries as high as 20,000 rubles. To put these numbers in perspective, a kilogram of meat or chicken was about 1,300 rubles. If a person ate only bread, then a monthly salary of 5,000 rubles would barely buy three pieces of bread per day in a month's period of time. Consequently, extended families would often pool their incomes so that if both husband and wife were working, and if the pensions of the parents were included, collectively they might achieve a subsistence income of 10,000–15,000 rubles. With a salary of 15,000 rubles, a mother reported the following: "I would buy a half kilogram of cheese and a quarter kilogram of butter per week, and the rest would be spent for bread." She reported also, "We don't buy new clothes anymore . . . all the money goes for food."

Of course, people inevitably had expenses other than food, such as those related to medication and childbirth. A grandmother reported that she experienced the worst day of her life a week before her daughter's child was due. She said that her daughter came home and started crying, saying that there was no money for her delivery. "Her crying really broke my heart," she said. So the family assured her that no matter what occurred they would support her. "After everything was over, the doctor asked for 10,000 rubles, and that's one month's earnings. Well, we were grateful that her husband's parents paid most of it, and we paid about 4,000 rubles ourselves. And she needed other care, like nurses and all, so the whole thing came to 12,000 rubles." Others were not so fortunate, especially if they had ongoing expenses related to medication. One woman reported that her husband's medication cost 35,000 rubles, which was simply out of the question, so he had to do without it and risk dying. Another person said that even 4,000 a month for medication was prohibitive for her, because it was a choice between bread and pills.

The combination of lack of medical care, inadequate nutrition, and living in severe cold, month after month, claimed many lives, which also meant that people had to be buried. Among Armenians, burial is an important rite of passage that involves inviting family and friends to commemorate the deceased person over a lavish meal. One woman said that they had sold their car for 100,000 rubles to have money to live on, but a quarter of that went to pay for the burial of her husband. Another woman said that she sold some of the furniture in her house and then borrowed money from friends to bury a loved one. But as people became poorer, they struggled even to find wood to build a casket, let alone bury their relatives with dignity. Consequently, the community would often band together: "My husband's cousin died of a heart attack. The family did not have money to bury him, so all of us got together. Some of us gave food; some of us gave money to get the casket. Some of us gave food so that we could have a dinner for all those who came to the funeral. It was sad, but that was the only way."

Given the high levels of unemployment and the fact that even working people barely made a subsistence wage, people sold any available asset: vases, silver spoons, china. When we asked a refugee from Nagorno-Karabakh how he was dealing with the financial crisis, he said, "To be honest, we have no money at all. We sold all our jewelry, our gold teeth, watches, and everything possible." Many personal assets, however, did not command much value in the depressed market of Armenia, as noted by a young mother: "I have done a lot of hand work. I have rugs and tablecloths and things like that, but I don't even think about selling them because how can someone buy tablecloths or a rug if he doesn't have enough money for bread?"

Not everyone was poor, of course. A few people had found ways of making money by importing goods from Iran or Russia. Anyone who looked really prosperous was labeled a member of the mafia. Charges of corruption within government, such as receiving foreign aid and then selling it to an impoverished population or diverting aid for military use, occurred frequently. A bright young woman analyzed the situation as follows: "In our country we now have two classes: the very rich and the very poor. The very rich families are able to purchase everything, including ultramodern clothes and cars; they only think about their pocket, and I don't think this is right. I feel that with their money they need to reach out to the poor and not think only about their pockets." Statistically, perhaps 5 percent of the population could be considered relatively well off; another 10–15 percent lived adequately; 50–60 percent lived under bad economic conditions; and roughly 25 percent lived in extreme poverty.

For many people, the only way to make an adequate living was to work outside Armenia and send money home. Some people even tried to engage in trade between Armenia and nearby countries, but on a small scale these endeavors often failed to produce a steady income. For example, one individual collaborated with friends and imported gasoline from Iran, making several dollars a gallon profit. Another individual exported inlaid sculptures with some success. The common person who tried to be entrepreneurial, however, typically was plagued by a lack of materials. For example, a widow said, "I used to make dolls, cute little dolls, for weddings, and I used to sell them, but then there was no material left. No material left to continue that craft that I used to do."

The problem, however, went far beyond the level of the individual craftsman. The entire Soviet system was built on the concept of interdependence—that no republic could exist without depending on the others. Armenia had an enormous sock factory that supplied much of the Soviet Union, but it depended on other republics for the raw material from which to weave socks. Furthermore, when the centralized Soviet economy collapsed, the marketing structure also disappeared. Who was going to buy the socks produced by Armenia, even if the raw material was available? And even had there been a marketing structure, factories in Armenia ceased to operate because of a lack of electricity, and once they had been idle for a few years, the technology had changed. So once again, even if Armenia had energy and raw materials, it had difficulty competing in the world marketplace.

In the years immediately after independence, everyone seemed to be buying and selling: children, scientists, and common laborers. There was nothing else to do. A woman offered this example of her husband's employer: "It's sad, really sad. Former engineers are now selling goods. My husband's former boss is selling soap. My husband said he saw him the other day, and he just changed the direction of his walk and didn't want his boss to see him. So many people are resorting to selling menial things, doing menial tasks because there is no work. They've lost their jobs." One person we interviewed estimated that almost no one was working up to their skill level. "I would say that only 2 percent work in their own specialty. Ninety-eight percent do not. They will do other jobs—whatever is available, but not in their specialization, in their majors, in the education that they got." For example, we bought hand-painted greeting cards from a highly skilled scientist, because this was the only means he had of making a little bit of income.

Many people we interviewed recognized that an economy cannot exist over the long term unless it is engaged in manufacturing. "Our country is boiled down to buying and selling. That's all we're doing. Buying and selling. Nothing else. And if any nation does just that, it will perish." In

Buying and selling goods became the main commercial enterprise after Armenia's industrial and scientific base collapsed. A young man displays goods in Yerevan.

fact, while outside aid was appreciated, this assistance simply perpetuated a situation of dependency, adding little to a self-generating economy. A scientist said,

> I'm thankful for foreign organizations that are giving us handouts. I'm not against it. There are people that are at the brink of starvation and, of course, it's needed. [But] what I think would be more profitable is if these foreign organizations would help us establish work, business. Help us to do something, produce something, and, as a result, make money. I wish the efforts would go toward that. Instead of just giving food, we would get machinery or whatever, and we would know how to use it and become productive. To me, that's the answer.

And a young woman said,

> I'm not against Armenians helping us from the diaspora. But I am for them helping us create opportunities for work, because we are a hard-working people. Unless we work hard, we cannot get back up on our feet again. So we need help in establishing, starting, and providing opportunities for us to work. That is the best way to help us: Create work opportunities so that we can work and make our own living.

Unfortunately, as an engineer told us, the consequences of breaking with the Soviet Union were not realized at the time of independence:

> Independence is real when a nation is both economically and politically independent. When we declared our independence, we meant only political independence. No one had thought about economic independence at that time. No one had thought about what would happen to us after we rejected the socialist economic system. I, too, was unable to predict such things. Now, I believe that it was a great mistake for all republics to declare themselves independent. We are in chaos now.

This realization emerged from his analysis of the company for which he worked. "We were the first republic in the Soviet Union to manufacture car stereos. And what does our organization do now? About four thousand people were fired because orders from other republics stopped. We have this amazing technology, and all we do now is produce locks."

The importance of having a job was revealed very subtly to us during a visit to a middle-class family. Everyone was home, including the kids and grandparents. The children were vivacious and entertained us. Their mother was a talented musician and played the piano. But in an alcove in the home lay the father—a good-looking man—asleep on a couch in the middle of the day. He was not exhausted from work. He was shutting out the reality of feeling worthless. When we asked one woman how her husband felt about his employment status, she said, "Whenever there is work for him, he is in a happy mood. Whenever there is no work for him, he is in a bad mood." Even more poignantly, a woman, speaking about herself, tied employment to her own sense of self-worth: "A job not only rewards a person financially, it also makes people feel needed by our society. I feel useless without a job. I have neither moral nor financial satisfaction now." For the employed, low salaries affect their self-esteem. A policeman with a small baby said, "It just causes me a heartache that I don't make any more, but I need to adjust. I need to adapt, reconcile, and look for solutions. But it comforts me on the other hand that at least I have a job, and others don't even have that."

Prior to independence, Armenia was one of the most affluent republics, and education was extremely valued by the population. But what do these people do with their degrees when the infrastructure of their country crumbles? One son said to his mother that he had two advanced degrees, but unfortunately they could not eat either one of them. These employment frustrations, as well as the sheer desperation of supporting a family, led many people to seek employment outside the country. One man said, "Last year I went to Russia, and there were six of us who went there. We went there to look for work, and we found work. We stayed for three months—August, September, and October. We worked there and made money, and we came back and used it to support our families." Another man said, "In the summertime I left the country three times. I went to Lithuania and Poland, where I made some money, which helped us to save for the winter." Other people left Armenia because they realized that they might not survive another winter:

> I am afraid next winter will be worse. That is why we are moving to Russia. We won't have enough preserves. We used all that we had last winter, and for this winter we cannot prepare any preserves because we don't have the means. We are planning to pass the winter, my wife and I, in Russia, and from there we can send goods to my parents so that they can survive the winter here.

Another consequence of an economy in such shambles is that people decide they cannot afford to marry. Still others decide they cannot afford to bring children into this world. A further unfortunate consequence is that some people withdraw from social contact. For example, a teacher told us that her clothes were so threadbare that she was ashamed to meet her students in public. Others said that they quit inviting friends over to socialize because they had nothing to offer them to eat. One man even told his wife that maybe they should consider committing a crime so that they would be put in jail. At least they would be fed there, he said.

Keeping Warm

During the winter, the temperature in a typical house was 5–6 degrees centigrade when the occupants had no means to heat their homes. In houses that were not well insulated, the situation was even more severe. One man said, "We had ice on our ceiling. We were very surprised that we survived. Our door was completely covered with ice. All of our drinking water was frozen." With the aid of electricity and wood or kerosene stoves, houses might warm up to 15–20 degrees, but this was often for only a brief period, because then the electricity would go out or people would let fires die down to conserve precious fuel. Sometimes it would be warmer outside than inside their homes. Houses made of stone seemed to retain heat best, but many apartments apparently had little insulation. Architects of Soviet-style buildings had not anticipated energy shortages.

To conserve heat, people would typically block off all but one room and congregate there during the day. When families retired for the night, they would wear several layers of clothes, including hats and overcoats, heaping their beds high with quilts and comforters. People commonly doubled up in the same bed. When a refugee from Baku was asked about the temperature in his house, he said, "To tell you the truth, I didn't measure it. But, to give you an idea, we slept *under* the mattress, not *on* it." As a tactic for staying warm, many people spent an inordinate amount of time in bed. Accounts like the following of being in bed for fourteen hours were not uncommon in our interviews: "We would go to bed at 8 P.M. and get up at 10 A.M. We just had to stay in bed a long time. That was the only way we could keep warm." An elderly woman from Nagorno-Karabakh described the same experience: "Many times I would stay in bed for a few days. That was the only way I could stay warm." And, expressing her strong memories of the cold, an engineer said, "Every time I remember those cold winter days I tremble and I feel as though I am really cold again. Our homes were awful. Most of the time we spent in our beds with layers and layers of clothing. The only thing we didn't have on was our shoes." Some people developed what they called a cold allergy: "very dry skin which frequently turns blue, and some bruises appear on it and don't heal for a long time."

To combat the cold people purchased stoves or sometimes built their own, such as one that an ingenious individual constructed out of a used paint can. But allocating money for a stove was not easy for many people. A woman from Nagorno-Karabakh said, "We had to cut down on our food, to the point of fasting, so I could save some money, about three thousand rubles, to buy a stove." Then the problem was where to find fuel to burn in these stoves. One mother said, "I burned paper, shoes, Russian books that I didn't need anymore. For example, my husband wasn't home one time, and there was no wood around the house and we were cold, so I just burned books that I had used in the past. Russian books. It was enough to warm ourselves up so we could go to bed." Another woman said, "Well, we burned two or maybe three doors from within the house. We had two old chairs, and we convinced my mother, and she gave up and we burned those. They were all of good, strong wood, so they gave us better heat."

Wood was a precious commodity, and many Armenians were highly ambivalent about cutting down trees. Apologetically, a man in his thir-

Everything was burned during winter, from Russian books to tires. This woman burns a piece of a tire in Yerevan.

ties said, "I am ashamed to say that twice I had to go and cut branches off live trees. And I know that wasn't the right thing to do, but I had to. You see, my sister was living with us with her child, and we had to care for the child and keep the place warm." An elderly man, nearly eighty, expressed the same ambivalence: "It was sad to see people uprooting trees. It really bothered me to see uprooting. They had a good reason, they wanted to stay warm, but uprooting was unnecessary. Others were more careful; they would only cut branches rather than the whole tree, leaving the roots in so it could grow back." Other people made a point of going to the forests or parks and gathering only twigs and branches that had fallen. Sometimes this was the task of children, but one person also reported the following: "Once I saw this really old lady, and she was collecting the tiny branches fallen down from cut trees. That's all she could carry to take home and keep warm." And some people, on principle, refused to place themselves in the position of using wood to stay warm: "I was offered a heater with wood, but I did not accept it, because I am against cutting trees. I said that just as others have survived, I will survive, too, without a stove or a heater that uses only wood."

When we drove through some of the mountainous regions outside of

Youth gathering branches from forest near Yerevan.

Yerevan, we saw entire hillsides that had been cut bare. For some this work was their employment; others simply took the opportunity to scavenge.

> We had a lousy wood stove. It needed wood. So we would go to the forest, and big, huge, capable men would topple the trees. They would carry the whole thing to their home, and we would get the fallen branches. My husband and I would carry the branches home. This was exhausting work, especially for my husband. He would perspire all the way. We didn't have the means nor could we ask anyone to haul it to our home. We did it ourselves.

This same woman said, "I wish there was a warm place where I could go sit and beg, just beg." But then she added, "You see how low we can get psychologically in these conditions."

Aid organizations provided heaters and kerosene, but this appears to have been a stopgap measure, according to people we interviewed. For one thing, the rules enforced in some areas allowed fuel rations only for those who had more than two children. This policy clearly angered people with one or two children, who nevertheless were cold. Also, when kerosene distributions occurred, supplies were exhausted within a few days. A scientist expressed his frustration, saying, "Now December has passed

Grandmother and grandson team up to collect fuel in Yerevan.

and it's January, and we are still not getting fuel. Our heaters that use fuel just sit like useless appliances in the house—not used because of lack of fuel." An elderly woman expressed disappointment with her mayor: "We were told that kerosene was going to be distributed here. The winter is almost over, and I've only received it once." On the other hand, some of the indigenous ways worked best. Armenians on farms often burned cow dung. One person living near a farm said, "We used to follow the cows and collect it that way." Other people invented their own solutions: "We wanted to buy a heater, but we realized it was too expensive, and we didn't know where to store the fuel. So I created a heating system with pipe. It's just enough to heat food and heat the water for tea."

Electricity and Water

The major source of electrical power prior to independence was the Medzamor nuclear power plant built by the Soviet government. Two interrelated events led to a decision to shut it down: first, the earthquake of 1988 and, second, the fear that Yerevan might be the site of another

Chernobyl. When the plant was closed, the blockade was not in effect, and undoubtedly no one foresaw the potential calamity that would occur without energy. Who would have imagined that a few years after this preventative measure was taken Armenians would be reduced to living like their medieval ancestors? In the absence of electric power, modern industrial society comes grinding to a halt, and this is precisely what happened in Armenia. Elevators in high-rise apartments did not operate. Water had to be carried. There were massive layoffs in industry. People sat in darkness at night. Public transportation ceased or became exorbitantly expensive.

Prior to the blockade the plan was to get power from neighboring republics and to produce electricity from gas-powered plants. However, the blockade cut off all points of access except through Georgia, Armenia's neighbor to the north, and, unfortunately, the gas pipeline was extremely vulnerable to attack by neighboring Azeri military forces. Hence, power outages frequently occurred because the pipeline supplying gas had been blown up. Sometimes it could be fixed in a few days, and other times it took much longer. In addition, our interviewees often mentioned that power lines were down, and neighbors sometimes took up collections to fix them. Apparently, local officials operating the electricity grid were occasionally bribed. For example, one of our research assistants asked a scientist whether money had been collected in his neighborhood, and he said, "Yes, but it did not work," which he blamed on the inflation that occurred between the time the money was gathered and when officials were petitioned for more electricity. "I see some neighborhoods have lights, so it is possible to get light, but collecting money is not working out in our neighborhood."

When electricity did come, residents had to prioritize their activities, knowing that it would probably not last for long. One woman described the bustle in their house in the middle of the night. "A couple of days ago, the electricity came on at 2 A.M. We all got up and did all kinds of chores. It was only one hour, and we had to cook, clean, and wash. One hour is too short. You can't do much. But we were all working like soldiers." Another woman was more pessimistic about how much could be done in a short period of time. "You can do one thing. You can do washing, heating your tea, preparing dinner. So you decide. When the electricity comes, this is what I'm going to do. You can do one thing and that's all." And another woman graphically described the choices she made: "I would bathe one day at a time: arms one day, legs another day, hair another day. It was impossible to take a bath all at once because of the cold. Same with cooking. We would only get about fifteen minutes a day, and I would cook a meal in three or four days: fifteen minutes one day, fifteen minutes another day, until it was cooked." When the power went off, life returned to its medieval state. A man with young children said, "Five minutes after the electricity was turned off, our place became as cold as a refrigerator."

On the other hand, when the power returned, everyone celebrated. An elderly woman described the response of her grandchildren: "They jump for joy when the light comes on." And a young mother offered this example of the effect of light: "One evening it was getting dark and I hadn't lit the candles yet, and my little daughter was restless and crying, and I thought there was no reason for her to cry. As soon as I lit the candles she was so happy. I realized that one little candle makes her happy. Can you imagine?" Candles, however, were often used sparingly, depending on the family's income level. "One candle will cost twenty or twenty-five drams, which is 15–20 percent of your salary. One candle only lasts two days." This need to prioritize resources often left people in complete darkness at night, which is one reason that many families went to bed shortly after sundown. This took its toll on students, however, who were unable to study at night. And it adversely affected many others, including one inventor, who said, "The hardest thing for me is darkness at night. You see, I like to work at night as well, but when it is dark, it is hard. I have to work with a lamp or candles. I cannot stop working."

The lack of electricity certainly had a profound effect on people's mood. However, one optimist told the following, perhaps apocryphal, story to make the point that one can find a silver lining in most misfortunes.

> A woman from the United States asked her counterpart in Armenia why the women she encountered were so sad. The Armenian woman answered, "We're not sad." But the woman from the U.S. said, "Yes, we see you are sad." So the Armenian woman had a question to ask the woman from the U.S.: "When our light comes on we are very happy. When your light comes on, are you happy?" The woman from the U.S. said, "No." The Armenian woman said, "When we get bread, we are very happy. When you get bread, are you happy?" The U.S. woman said, "No." The Armenian woman continued, "When we get water, we are very happy. When you get water, do you get happy?" The U.S. lady said, "No." The Armenian lady then concluded, "See, we are happier than you are."

Nevertheless, the lack of electricity affected every aspect of life for Armenians after independence. If Armenian society had not already reached an advanced, urbanized state, then coping with the cold might not have been so difficult. For example, Armenians living in eastern Turkey in the early part of the twentieth century sometimes kept their cows on the ground floor of their houses so that the cows would keep warm and, in turn, their warmth would rise to the stories above. Furthermore, houses were built to hold the heat in, whereas much Soviet-style housing was not well insulated, in part because residents didn't pay for their electricity—it was supplied by the state. In addition, people were not acculturated to living in the dark; hence, to be thrust back into such a primitive state was as traumatic as not having enough to eat. Indeed, one man said, "Energy is more important at this point in our history than is bread."

The lack of electricity affected not only heating and cooking, but also all activities associated with water. Because the pumps that delivered water to houses and high-rise apartments did not work much of the time, people often had to carry their water, sometimes from considerable distances. One person, for example, indicated that he carried his water from "three bus stops" away. People whose pipes were not broken from the freezing temperatures collected water in bathtubs, buckets, kettles, and pans. Families with babies had an especially difficult time trying to wash diapers. One woman said that she gave up washing clothes during the winter and simply waited until spring. Hospitals not only found it very difficult to maintain adequate heat and to provide light for surgery and nursing, but they were also affected by the irregular flow of water required to maintain hygienic facilities. And a mother said that lice got into her children's hair, and, without regular access to warm water, it was extremely difficult to get rid of them.

Transportation

The same factors that led to cold homes and lack of food also affected the transportation industry. The buses, metro, and streetcars ran very irregularly. Even if they were operating, many people could not afford to ride them. Driving a car was nearly out of the question for the average person; most people had either sold their vehicles or could not afford to operate them. Consequently, people usually walked everywhere they went. An older woman, for example, said that she walked an hour each way to work. The sick found it difficult, if not impossible, to reach medical care. One woman said that her ninety-two-year-old mother was bleeding heavily one day, and she called a doctor, but he said that he could come to visit her only if she provided him with a ride. Emergency departments were nearly nonfunctional. A doctor said, "We didn't have fuel, so how could we go and rescue the urgent care patients? And how will the patients understand that the doctor is late? I have been called to homes where kids have already died. Lives could have been saved if we had had the means—the emergency car, the fuel— [to reach the patients]."

A medical student offered the following perspective on the difficulty of pursuing her studies:

> Transportation for many students attending university was very difficult. I was still a medical student, and the hospitals, unfortunately, are on the outskirts of the city, and I had to travel. I often, of course, tried to go on the trolley, but often they were stopped because of the lack of energy. For that reason, I often had to walk, even in my pregnant condition. Often there would be snow and ice, and the cold would be severe, but I had to go. I did, though, develop bronchitis, and I missed school for two weeks, and it was very crucial.

Other people were unable to observe family and ritual obligations. One woman said, "I could not visit my father's grave, because buses don't work and I could not afford a taxi. For several months I haven't visited his grave." Another woman said, "I couldn't even wish my mom a happy New Year. My dad died three years ago, and my mom lives in the village, and I haven't seen her for several months. I couldn't afford to go. I don't know if I will ever see her. You see, every penny counts, and we have to save for our daily bread. I dream about her every night though."

Illness

Illness was predictable, given the poor nutrition and cold environment that many people experienced. A woman said that her mother-in-law's sister was only thirty-five when she died. She had volunteered to stand in a bread line for the family and had become extremely chilled. This was not uncommon. Many people contracted pneumonia, and the mortality rate was high because people could not be cared for properly once they became ill. One person observed that a number of people who survived the winter, especially heart patients, died in the spring from their weakened condition. Even children were susceptible to lingering illnesses that would have been contained easily with adequate care and nutrition.

One mother pragmatically addressed the cause, saying, "How do you expect a kid to be healthy when you are feeding him vermicelli with some tomato sauce day in and day out? How do you expect that kid to be healthy? Our children are weak. I am worried about them." This same woman commented on the death of one of her in-laws, who had a weak heart: "The cold was the main cause of death. The other fact was that the food was so scarce. So he just did not make it." Parenthetically she added, "My fear is that next winter many will not make it for the same reasons."

How many people died from cold and inadequate nutrition is an open question. A retired historian said that she knew of ten people who had died: "Some in their forties, some in their fifties, and some very young children." She said, "I myself had the flu, and I was very sick, and I'm thankful that I made it." One woman said that she remained healthy during the winter but commented, "Under these conditions you have to be made out of stone to stay healthy."

Physical elements were not alone in taking their toll; psychological stress also played a role:

What can I say? It was a very difficult winter. It was an incredibly severe winter. It definitely affected people's psychological state. My father was very ill, and it wasn't healthy for him to breathe that air near our stove. We were looking for wood and were carrying that wood to the eleventh floor—the elevator was never working. He had been breathing that air and coughing frequently. It was cold and he also had bronchitis. He was very sick, and he needed to stay warm and to breathe clean air. His doctor told us that his condition was serious. She said that he needed to stay in a hospital, but it was too cold to let him stay in a hospital. Here, at least, we had a stove. Because of the temperature in our apartment, however, he got a cold. It wasn't only the cold that killed him. He was very nervous and he suffered a lot. He was upset watching us suffer.

A doctor we interviewed summarized the situation, saying, "There are psychological problems, stress, nervousness, heart conditions, hypertension, kidney problems—all because of the conditions of today." He said that in one extended family, he had seen three people die within a month.

Pregnancy

Considerable ambivalence was expressed regarding pregnancy and the prospect of responsibly raising children in this society. One mother of two said, "I think any intelligent woman should not be pregnant. Or, if pregnant, she should terminate it, because there is no food. It is not possible to raise a child today. The conditions are such that you cannot raise a child, so it is unwise to bring children into this world." Others were less pessimistic, especially if they could afford an adequate diet: "It is wise for any mother-to-be to have a good diet before she becomes pregnant. If she decides to be pregnant, she has to have a good diet. So, having that in mind, one can go ahead with that plan. If one cannot afford that kind of diet, one should not be pregnant."

The problems of caring for newborn infants in these conditions were described by those who had recently given birth. "Well, I don't have enough milk to nurse her, so we need additional milk, but there isn't any. Time and again we have gone and asked, and they say it will come, but it doesn't come." In response to our question about how the baby was doing, the mother said, "We give her tea, but it doesn't seem to satisfy her." Outside aid did reach some people. A policeman with a new infant said, "Now he has powdered milk. This milk was given by the United States and also by the Red Cross from France and Germany, and all young children are now taken care of because of this assistance that we get from abroad."

When asked whether they planned to have more children, parents often said no. One woman who had lost a child in the earthquake said bluntly, "We cannot afford to have any more." And a gynecologist summarized the situation saying, "Of course, we have fewer births now because of the conditions." She was against abortion, even though times were hard: "Yes, these pregnant women who come to us, they do suffer because of lack of electricity, heat, and water. Yes, it is a hard time for them." But, in spite of this, she said with regard to abortion, "Yes, it is done, and it is legal, and many women do undergo it, but I feel that it is life, and that they are taking a life."

Everyday Life

Given the social and economic conditions, how did people pass their days during the winter? If they had any source of heat at all, they typically made tea in the morning. Whoever was employed left for work, and the others pursued their chores, which typically included hauling water, looking for wood, and doing whatever shopping was required for the day. Women would handle the normal responsibilities of cleaning and maintaining the household. Sometimes they would bake bread, if they had flour, and they would, of course, prepare meals subject to the limitations of available electricity. Children, because they often were not in school during the winter, would bundle up and play outside, go to the park, or play games at home. A mother said, "When times were such that we could get out, I did. I took the children, and they went sliding on the snow." But when asked if her children had toys, another mother replied, "No, how could we have toys? There were a couple of broken items. That's what they used to play with. But otherwise they would just touch each other, play with each other, just love each other. That's about it."

Many things took longer than usual to do because of the lack of transportation. One family turned the baby stroller into a wagon for carrying wood, food, and other items. Many people said that they were bored. One woman who had been out of work for a year said, "Physically it's restful, but emotionally and spiritually it is frustrating." And a woman said about her husband, "He reads most of the time, smokes, looks for a job, feels frustrated. I comfort him and tell him that all is going to be well." Another woman said, "I did my daily chores. I also did embroidery, which made me feel good, because I was able to produce nice things." She also read the paper, but said that she tired of it "because they are writing a lot of lies." A refugee from Baku said, "Our only drive was to find something to burn to warm our children." In describing how her family spent their time, a woman said, "It was terrible: no TV, no radio, no lights. Nothing! All we could do was stare at each other. It was devastating and depressing. I was certain that we would get some serious psychological illnesses because of that. I often took my frustration out on my kids."

Teenagers and young adults found their lives dramatically altered. Not only were they not going to school, but the usual nightlife was absent. A young woman said, "In the old days, when I used to attend college, days were better. There was transportation; we always had activities at nights. We went to school during the day and enjoyed night activities. We can't do that anymore, and we can't complain, either, because these are the conditions we are under."

People did complain, however, about being cut off from cultural activities. A woman said, "During our years in the past, cultural events were very common for us—to attend theater, movies, concerts—but we have not seen that for many years now." Another person was more assertive when asked whether she went to the theater or engaged in any other type of entertainment: "No. Number one, they were closed, and, number two, if they were open there was no way we had any financial help to go. We both love music very much, but we can't engage in such a luxury."

Given the limited resources, people had to make their own music. In

Children use baby stroller to haul wood in winter near Yerevan.

the process of explaining how he tried to cope with his own depression, a man said, "At night, when it is dark, I've decided with my wife to bring out my guitar and play and sing. My wife sings and my son sings, and it cheers us up." In addition, he said, they sometimes invited their neighbors to join them: "We sing both happy and sad songs. We sing both sacred and folk songs. We sing children's songs." He said that their singing made it easier to "overcome the darkness" at night. And through this experience, he said, they had become closer with their neighbors. "The children play and we talk. So we overcome the depression this way." An artist said that he would get together with other painters: "In the past we spent time enjoying one another, doing things for fun, attending cultural events, but these are past now. We no longer can afford it. We do talk, we do share thoughts, and things like that. Nothing luxurious. No unnecessary spending."

If there was a silver lining to the post-independence circumstances, it was that neighbors and extended families sometimes came closer together as they confronted their common problems. A twelve-year-old child said, "I think our family became tighter during the winter. We were home most of the time, so we would talk a lot." He also said that he got to know

Making music at home in Yerevan.

his grandmother better. Families would often gather in the home of whoever had a heater, and although space was crowded, they would share
the heat. A woman with a young baby said that every day she would go
stay with her mother for a few hours because her house was warmer.
Another man's wife and daughter moved in with her parents for the winter because they had a warmer house. And a photographer whose business had completely collapsed said,

> We have neighbors with whom we share the heat. Many are more fortunate
> than we are, so they invite us over. We go and share, and we visit. We have
> been close with our neighbors. We have been here for some twenty-two
> years in this neighborhood, and we have gotten very close, especially during
> this past couple of years, when the difficulties were many. We were able to
> get together, share, comfort one another, share whatever we had. So it
> enabled us to get really close to one another.

People in the community often helped each other out. One woman
said, "My husband used to help get wood for our neighbors so that they
could put it in their stove and heat the house." In turn, this family shared
the stove with their neighbors. When asked how relationships had
changed under these difficult conditions, a refugee from Baku who was

Photo studio in Yerevan.

living in a settlement outside of Yerevan said, "People became more nervous, more anxious." But then he quickly countered by saying, "The winter somehow united the people. For example, if I had some fuel and you had some fuel, we would get together and use all of it."

On the other hand, some people seemed to withdraw under the adversity. One woman said, "We hardly ever visited because it was just too cold. Once in a while we would see people, and we would greet them and just talk a little. But we never sat together and talked. No, we did not do that." Another person said, "Yes, I'd say that some people have become introverts, quiet, keeping to themselves. They don't like to relate to others. They don't trust others. They've forgotten the old hospitality of visiting one another. They keep to themselves." And a refugee from Baku who had lost both of her parents to illness said, "We even stopped communicating with our relatives. We were completely isolated from everybody else. And staying inside of this apartment was very depressing—just look at our burnt ceiling."

Obviously, people never respond uniformly to any situation. One man noted that there were always two types of people. "There were some who were withdrawn and would only care for themselves, and others just got together and supported one another and shared their goods with one another." A woman drew a different distinction between people: "I know of a young lady who is a very generous person, and when she walks on the streets or goes shopping and she sees needy people around her, she helps them. She gives them money. It's wonderful. On the other hand we have people who would rather steal the potato that you bought with the only money that you have. So we have both extremes in our country. I'm ashamed of the second." Sometimes that greed translated into outright corruption:

> I came home one day, and my wife had bought this meat. Special dried meat, sausage, and I said, "Where did you get this? I've never seen it before." And she said, "It came from the United States." I said, "From the United States! How come?" "Well," she said, "it's actually supposed to be for the victims of the earthquake, but they are selling it and it's so good, I bought it." And I thought, Where are our values? What are we doing? We call ourselves Christians. We call ourselves a Christian nation!

Although people gathered around stoves and heaters for warmth, economic conditions worked against the custom of casually visiting friends and neighbors. The cultural custom was to offer food to visitors and then to send them away with a gift. Unfortunately, many people did not have even the bare minimum of surplus food to offer. One poignant example is that of a woman's husband who invited home someone who had done them a favor. The fellow realized that they had no food to serve, so he said, "Don't worry. I don't expect you to give me anything. Just coffee will be enough." But, of course, the woman did not have coffee, either.

> So I went to my neighbor's house and I knocked on her door. It was late, but I hoped she'd wake up for me. Sure enough, she was up and said, "What do you want?" and I told her what was up. I was on this balcony and she was on the balcony too. She was passing this coffee to me, and it was difficult to reach, and I couldn't quite make it, and the coffee fell all the way down, three stories below.

The woman ended the story by saying, "Now I'm laughing, but at the time it was so embarrassing."

Who Fared the Worst?

Comparing suffering is always difficult, but we did ask who fared the worst during the winter and received fairly uniform responses. Consis-

Downtown Yerevan in winter. The elderly had the most difficult time.

tently, people said that the elderly had the hardest time. First, they were the most likely to become ill. Furthermore, those who were on pensions ended up with almost nothing to live on because of inflation. Also, if they lived alone, it was difficult for them to gather food or find a way to heat their homes. In addition, the elderly often felt helpless and disliked being a burden to their children because of their inability to be self-sufficient. The lack of transportation seriously affected their mobility. Finally, they simply had a harder time staying warm because of poor circulation and lower metabolism. A refugee from Baku said, "I can't describe how I feel when I see older women going through the trash. I don't understand why the pension for the people is not being delivered on time. Our senior citizens, having no help at all, having no other source of income for two to three months, receive no pension at all."

Somewhat to our surprise, scientists and scholars were mentioned as being hit hard by the winter. Not only did they suffer from the cold along with everyone else, but they were simultaneously robbed of their identity. Their skills were no longer useful, and they did not seem to be valued by the wider population. Survival depended on buying and selling, as well as on the manual labor associated with gathering wood. Their training and years of study—that which distinguished them in society—were of little value in a world that had been reduced to subsistence survival.

Refugees from Azerbaijan were also identified as a needy group. They arrived in Armenia with very few assets, even though many of them were well off in Baku or Sumgait. They had abandoned their homes, and often they had only what they carried with them when they fled. They lacked a reservoir of assets that they could liquidate, and their housing was often abysmal. Describing this population, an individual said: "Yes, some people managed to bring something with them, but I know a lot more refugees who lived in poverty. Their rooms had no heat at all, and they could not get any light, either. The doors and windows of their apartments were broken. I am amazed that they managed to survive."

The group that people seemed to think did the best was wealthy businessmen who profited from the need to import things into Armenia, although even they were said to complain about the circumstances. In addition, children were often noted as doing all right, in part because they lacked perspective on the calamity that was striking the nation and the livelihood of their parents. Also, people from the laboring class were viewed, at least by the intelligentsia, as surviving better than some others—because their skills were more easily transferred to buying and selling, wood gathering, and so on. Obviously, this may be a dubious, if not elitist, assumption, since the laboring class lacked the resources available to more affluent elements of the population. On the other hand, it is important to include loss of dignity and identity as important factors when assessing the impact of economic conditions on the scientific community and intellectual class.

We also asked whether men or women had a more difficult time during the winter, and most people responded that the stress was equal, although experienced differently. Men felt the burden of providing the family income, whereas women experienced the day-to-day challenge of preparing food, keeping things clean without adequate water, and caring for children. A dentist with two young children said, "The men have to worry about making ends meet and supporting the family. The women have to worry about the children all day long. My wife is only twenty-three years old, and she has so much to do: caring for the kids, housework, cleaning, cooking, and it's very difficult for her. Often I see her in tears." A young mother with a baby expressed in more detail what she felt:

> I think each one has her own burden to bear. Me, I used to be quite nervous, and often I felt that my husband didn't feel it. I use to feel very nervous to provide for the little one, to keep her warm, to wash her clothes, to feed her,

things like that. Every so often I would get the feeling that I would lose her. So I used to be uptight, and when the electricity came—the hour of electricity every day—I had a million things to do, wash, dry, cook. I used to be so uptight. I felt that I would do everything I could and when it would go off, I would feel relieved that, well, that's it, I can't do any more. On the other hand, my husband felt that he had to support our family. The burden of the family's well being is on his shoulders, and he's the breadwinner, and so he had his own concerns. He works hard to provide for us. So each one of us has her or his own burdens to bear.

She ended by saying, "But beyond all this we love each other, and we're content in that regard."

Personality differences clearly contribute to the way people handle stress, so distinctions based on gender are problematic. For example, one woman said, "I would say that I am stronger than my husband. I can stand the conditions much better than he does." Another woman pointed to the emotional pressures that men feel as the breadwinners: "To the man it's more psychological, because he needs to make a living for the whole household, and it's a constant pressure on him." On the other hand, women in Armenian society often worked, including many who were doctors and well-trained engineers and the like; thus, although the cultural focus may be on men as the breadwinners, when the economy was good, women contributed significantly to family income.

Another person made the point that the suffering experienced was a function of people's expectations: "I would say that those who had no difficulties in their prior lives, who had worked smoothly and without problems, when they came face-to-face with the difficulties, they really had a hardship. They could not adapt and reconcile, whereas those who had difficulties in their past and had gone through similar situations were able to face the difficulties and adjust." Although it may seem obvious, this point is important. One may be tempted to say that the suffering of Armenians cannot be compared, for example, with that of people in Ethiopia or other Third World countries that are faced with chronic drought or other problems. On the other hand, previous life experience does play a role, and we must recognize that Armenia is not a Third World country. People were highly educated, and they lived middle-class lives, mostly in cities. Hence, to be forced back into a medieval state was a shock—the shock that any of us would feel if we had to give up our computers, television sets, automobiles, running water, and central heating. As noted, people in the villages suffered less acutely—in part because they were able to live off the land. For example, they still used dung for fuel, had wells for water, and grew much of their own food. On the other hand, after several winters people did start to make adjustments. They bought stoves, they stockpiled food (if they could afford to), and many left the country if they had the means.

Another comparison we pursued was whether children or adults suffered more during the winter. While children lost weight and went hungry, sometimes to the point of crying themselves to sleep at night, they did not seem to experience the mental anguish of their parents and grandparents. This generalization is based on interviews with twenty-five children, ages five to fourteen, as well as the observations of parents about children. For example, an eight-year-old offered this set of generalizations:

> The winter was very cold. Whenever it was a little warmer, we would go outside to play. Most of the time we would play at home. I played with my friend Alina. We cuddled up in blankets to keep warm. Whenever there was electricity, we would put the electric plate on and sit right next to it. It made me sad when there was no electricity because it was very cold. . . . I didn't go to school. There was no school to go to. I just stayed home. I did some studying at home. I learned how to read and write, and memorized some poems at home. I helped my mother by doing the dishes and drying them. We carried water from outside. . . . We didn't have much food during the winter. For some time the cafeteria gave us food. It wasn't very good. Then we got some food in boxes, but we finished it all.

Many of the younger children seemed to live in the moment. If there was one thing they missed other than food and heat, it seemed to be television. Everybody appeared to brighten up when the lights came on and the television started working again. A grandmother observed about her grandchildren,

> When it's dark you feel low. When it's light you feel happy. This is the same with children as well. They are happy when there is light, and they get active, and they say, "Let's put on TV," and they hook up the television. Even we adults, we're happy when it's light. But when it's dark you just feel low, and all you think about is going to bed.

However, in lieu of TV some traditional modes of entertainment flourished. Parents told stories to their kids, taught them basic educational skills, and tried to figure out ways to entertain them.

> My older daughter played music, and my younger daughter did lessons. Neither could go to school for three months, December to March, so they had to do everything at home. We all adjusted. We all endured. This was

an unusually harsh winter. We didn't expect it. It's the worst winter that I
can say we had. We survived. We got together; we told stories, fables, tales,
and kept the hours occupied.

Another child of about six said, "When there was no story time on TV
because of lack of electricity, we would just go to sleep early. My mother
would play the piano and we would sing." This child even said, "It was
fun during the winter." A mother we interviewed refused to go that far
in her evaluation, but she did say, "As I teach them and as I help them
with their homework, I forget about my hardships and difficulties." Another woman, a single mom, said that it felt like she and her kids were
in prison together, but that was partly because of the cultural deprivation they experienced: "It's unfortunate because the kids themselves are
in prison with me. What I mean is this. As I was growing up I always went
to the theater, I always went to the movies, I always participated in cultural activities. But my children now are deprived of it. They have nowhere to go because of the lack of fuel, lack of electricity."

The real cultural change, however, was that children were forced into
activities that contradicted Armenian values. With a heavy heart a
mother with three children described seeing two kids begging in the
metro:

> It really grieved me when I saw that. It's very hard for me to see beggars.
> I gave them fifty drams, but what's fifty drams? It's hard to see such pov-
> erty. Also on the streets you see young people with their little tables, buy-
> ing and selling. That's another sore point for me. I just feel sad for these
> children who are encouraged or forced to buy and sell, or are only interested
> in that, and have no interest in education.

A college-age student compared his experience with that of these children, saying that he was healthy and carefree as a youth, but "today's
children are unhealthy. They are thin, and some of them are forced to
steal bread to survive. It's tragic."

Some of the people we interviewed worried about what the long-term
impact would be on this generation of youth that is being deprived of
education and forced to learn survival skills that compromise their civic
consciousness. "I look at those kids and think of their future. They are
manning those tables, yes, buying and selling. What is going to happen
to them in the future? What kind of leaders will they be? What kind of
adults will they be? What kind of husbands, fathers will they be? It really breaks my heart."

Survival Attitudes

It is easier to generalize about the social and economic conditions that Armenians experienced than about the ways in which they coped with these conditions and the factors that led to different responses and attitudes. Nevertheless, two basic clusters of responses emerged clearly. First, there were people who seemed overwhelmed by their circumstances and expressed feelings of melancholy, resignation, and depression. Second, there were those who seemed to fight off these emotions; they were hopeful, guardedly optimistic about the future, and tried to create a little bit of joy and happiness in the midst of very depressing conditions. The latter either had someone who gave them meaning and pushed them to move forward with hope and optimism or had some purpose for their lives that superseded the immediate struggle for survival. Those who were depressed and resigned allowed themselves to sink with their circumstances. The differences between these two groups of people cannot easily be ascribed to gender, age, or any other obvious factor.

A mother of three put it this way: "The day starts, and you don't know how to provide for the children. But you look at them. You see their expectant eyes, their total dependency on you, and somehow that gives you hope to create something for them." A mother with two teenage daughters said, "If it weren't for my kids, I don't think I could make it. My kids have given me the inspiration and the energy to keep going. For their sake I have kept going." And a father said that his mother comforted him—especially when he was out of work—but his children "energized" him. He said, "It's true. Their youth, their attitudes, just that they are little children, gives me energy." Obviously, sometimes the tables seemed to turn, and the children comforted the parents. An unemployed mother said her children would sometimes say to her, "Mom, all will be well. Don't worry."

A number of people, both parents and grandparents, had little hope that things would get better in their lifetime—or at least the immediate future—but they had faith in the nation. They felt that it would survive, partly because Armenians had faced hardships in the past, and they had always overcome them. They had been massacred, deported, and stripped of territory, and yet they still existed. This perseverance, this endurance, is what guarantees hope for future generations of Armenians and therefore for the children of the people we interviewed. One man we interviewed put it this way:

Grants from the Armenian General Benevolent Union supported the symphony orchestra in Yerevan during the worst of times.

You see, we have to have vision and we have to have a light—illuminated vision—otherwise life becomes meaningless. So we have this vision that we are going to make it, and we are going to be a strong nation, and we're going to be a productive nation, and we're going to work for that. We have this dream. We've got to live with this dream. Otherwise life doesn't make sense.

Another person tried to put a positive spin on the sufferings of Armenians: "Difficulties train you and make you a better person." Because of the social and economic conditions, this woman said that they stayed home and appreciated their neighbors. In addition, she said, "I read more, I thought more, and I know I matured more. Mentally I was happy." Another person, who said that she typically looks on the bright side of things, stated, however, that the conditions were "turning optimists into pessimists and civilized people into barbarians." We did hear many complain that people had become more self-centered, simply looking after their own survival. An unemployed man who had been wounded in the war said that people used to be more respectful: "They minded one another. Now things have changed. People are more indifferent, more self-centered. The culture has kind of gone down. Yes, it is much different

Returning home in Yerevan

now." An older woman explained how she had been robbed in broad daylight by someone who demanded her necklace and her purse. On the other hand, another person said it was understandable that people would steal so that they and their families could eat.

This movement toward incivility perhaps went hand in hand with the general cultural deprivation that many people felt. A woman with several sons said, "How can anyone think about art, music, literature when one only thinks about food?" At the same time, a few fortunate individuals who lived near the opera house in Yerevan took advantage of the free (or nearly free) concerts, and one woman credited her survival to being able to attend these events. "The only one who saved our lives was Jeknavorian, our symphony conductor. I wasn't able to go to some of his performances, but he was the only one who kept us going." Others found strength by comparing their suffering to what their fellow Armenians were experiencing in Nagorno-Karabakh: "This kind of living cannot be called 'comfortable,' of course, but it is relative. We can take all this knowing that there are people who constantly live in a state of war, under fire. We are only freezing here. But there, children and other innocent people are dying at this moment."

The people who were most optimistic were those who gained strength from each other. Those who seemed most bitter were people who, for one reason or another, were isolated. Their network of support was diminished, and they were trying to make it through these difficulties on their own. While inner strength is important, it seems equally important to have relatives and neighbors with whom to bond and share the load.

5

"We Live with Hope"

Reflections on Conditions in Armenia

Near the end of one of our interviews, a scientist turned to our research assistant and indicated that he had some reflections for the people conducting this research project. He wanted us to know that Armenia might be experiencing some difficult times, but that spring inevitably follows winter, and there was every reason to be hopeful about the future. He believed that Russia, America, Azerbaijan, and Armenia should all sit down together and negotiate an end to the war. In his view, peace would bring prosperity back to the land. Why? Because while Armenia might not have an abundance of resources, it did have highly educated, well-trained, creative people: "We have this vision that we are going to make it and we are going to be a strong nation and we're going to be a productive nation." Citing Armenian national character, he said, "I know that we are a people that can survive, endure, produce, manufacture." To justify this optimism, he pointed to the long history of Armenians, going back even before the birth of Christ. "We are the remnant of this great nation," he said. "We can't quit. We can't give up. We can't end it." He appealed to the model of Israel, with Jews scattered all over the globe.

Armenians are similar, he said. "We've got to stick to our history, to our country, and we've got to maintain and keep this nation going." In his view, people must live with hope.

The preceding chapters have focused on personal narratives of people who struggled through the winters in Yerevan, survived the earthquake, were affected by the war in Nagorno-Karabakh, or fled from Azerbaijan because of the pogroms. In this chapter we suggest some cross-cutting themes that surfaced in all four populations that we interviewed: (1) assessments of Armenia's future, (2) political views on governance, (3) reflections on solving Armenia's energy problem, (4) the decision to stay in Armenia or emigrate, and (5) historical comparisons between the current situation and earlier crises in Armenia's past. However different these issues may be, they all demonstrate how common citizens wrestle with the larger issues of human meaning and political policy.

Armenia's Future

Not everyone whom we interviewed shared the optimism of the scientist just cited. Several people said that patience had its limits. One man said that it is possible to be patient for one year, perhaps even two or three years, but after that one starts to run low on hope. Another individual offered a slightly longer time frame but still said there were limits: "Two years ago I thought that we could survive only one more year like that. However, it has been two years and we survived. I do not really know what the breaking point will be. A human being can take a lot—a year, two years, three years, five years—but I am not certain about longer periods of time." We frequently heard Armenians cite endurance as a national character attribute. Sometimes it was associated with the 1915 genocide and the fact that even though half the Armenians in Turkey lost their lives, the nation still endures. Another person said tersely, "Armenians survive. Armenians endure." Still another said, "I feel sorry for the Armenians. Armenians have always suffered. They've always had hardships. They've been wanderers in this world, but somehow I know they endure. We will persevere. We can endure no matter how much the odds are against us." Far from being fatalistic, people felt that hardship inevitably came to Armenians, but they would not succumb. They are a people whose belief in survival is solidly grounded, even if it takes rather stoic forms. One elderly woman summarized her situation by saying, "I am still standing," which is not a particularly optimistic statement but does indicate forbearance.

Many people had given up on their own future, especially if they were elderly. They acknowledged that it would take years for Armenia to make an economic recovery. Their hope was based on the future of their children and grandchildren. An elderly woman said, "I am concerned about the welfare of the children. They've got to have a future. They count." Another woman realistically said, "I'm sixty-one and I'm not that strong, either, so I doubt if I will make it myself." Nevertheless, she had faith, stating not once but twice, "I have not lost my faith." Others were more careful in expressing their optimism. Several people said that they were delaying childbirth. Indicating the basis for her choice, a young married woman said, "I couldn't face my child in the future if he blamed me for bringing him into this world—to this difficult and unbearable world." Another person contrasted his childhood with that of children living in Armenia today: "When I observe how our youth spend their time, I become upset and hurt. It's impossible to compare my youth with theirs. We had a rich cultural and intellectual life. If our youth manage to go to a concert, then that day becomes a holiday."

The consensus of nearly everyone we interviewed was that if the war could be settled and the blockade lifted, Armenians would survive because of their fortitude and intelligence. A recently married man said, "I would say that I have no hope, but I can tell you that if the war ends, we will be okay. The Armenians are industrious and intelligent. If the war ends, within two years I know that we can be back to normal. We can get back on our feet again." Some people, however, did not qualify their lack of hope. One man said, "If it continues this way, I have no hope. People don't have food, they don't have work, they're starving. This cannot go on." And a woman who confessed to frequently crying said, "I can't complain. I am too weak to complain. I'm too depressed."

Other people feared that the national character had been altered by the hardship of the past few years. People were no longer generous, and they no longer entertained. They only looked after their own self-interest. Even worse, people were becoming violent, and they were stealing and assaulting in ways that never had occurred prior to independence, when life was more affluent. A man who was actually quite optimistic said, "When the conditions are bad, man's tendency is to do just that, become violent." Nevertheless, we also spoke with people who firmly believed that societal conditions need not dictate behavior. "In today's conditions, it is very difficult to retain all the human qualities people had before. But I believe that it is now that we must retain them. Now we must all be able to support each other. We need that. Now we cannot become isolated. We need to stay together and stay strong. We need to create better conditions for life here."

Although physical and economic circumstances undoubtedly contribute to people's ability to move beyond self-absorption, some of our interviewees showed a remarkable ability to surmount their personal situations. One woman said, "We have no right to complain about our minor everyday problems and the absence of comfort. At least we have a roof over our heads, we have a sofa and a few blankets under us so we can try to stay warm. It is not as bad as suddenly becoming homeless during a severe winter and losing our close ones." This woman held to a vision that everything would return to normal once the war ended. "And then our teachers will start teaching again, and others will return to their jobs again. We need to create the necessary conditions for our future generations to survive and flourish. In five or ten years, everything will be fine in Armenia again."

Political Critique

People were not hesitant, as they had been under communist rule, to speak their minds about the failures and successes of the government. Many people acknowledged that the transition to democracy and a capitalist economy was in its infancy, so it was important to exercise patience. Nevertheless, strong statements were made about the ineptitude of the Levon Ter-Petrossian administration during the 1993–94 period, when we conducted the interviews. While very few people wanted to return to communist rule, they sorely missed the law and order associated with the previous regime. They frequently charged that the new republic was in a state of anarchy. People complained of corruption within government, including collaboration with the mafia. They also feared that, however good independence sounded abstractly, a small republic like Armenia needed a strong alliance with Russia, especially given the hostility of Armenia's neighbors.

Many people cited specific examples of the current administration's ineptitude. The chaos surrounding the bread lines was viewed as one instance where the government should have exercised stronger leadership. Some typical comments follow:

Why aren't they organizing a simple thing like that [the bread lines]? I just do not understand. . . . Bread is so important to the Armenians. The least they can do is get organized and have enough bread for everyone so people can live normally, for goodness' sake.

The bread lines were very unorganized. Our whole government is unorganized. It is chaotic. Who can you complain to for your ills?

Look at the lines, the bread lines. The hundreds and thousands of people. Everyone needs to get in line to get bread. How humiliating! Look at our condition today. It has become total humiliation. When we have to stand in lines, day in and day out, to get lousy bread and the government just sits there. . . . What can I say about a government like that, which is so indifferent?

The same complaint was made about the distribution of fuel:

There is no law or order. You just go and try to get your kerosene. A young fellow tries to put you in queues. You wait all night and you wait the next day, and it's not there. Why not create order by calling certain areas of the city and saying, "You come. It's your day today to get kerosene," and make sense out of it. It's humiliating and it's ridiculous, and people take advantage of situations like this.

An even more frequent criticism was that fares on the public buses were not regulated by the government. Apparently, drivers often charged whatever the market would tolerate. The following comment was typical: "Prices rise uncontrollably. How can people live? In buses, they name any price they want. From here to the closest village, they charged me 150 rubles. How can they do that? There is no law!"

Others felt that the government should have played a stronger role in controlling the cutting of trees. If it was really necessary to cut trees to provide fuel for basic heating and cooking, then at least the government should have supervised this activity—providing some guidance as to what to cut. Instead, the government apparently simply sent soldiers demanding that people not cut trees at all, but this was unrealistic when people were freezing to death. One frustrated individual said, "They should be told to plant twenty trees if they are going to cut one tree down. We've got to have law and order. We can't go on like this in a chaotic mess."

In attempting to assess the lack of governance, one person stated that elected officials simply lacked experience. They knew how to promote the idea of independence, but the task of running a country was another matter. Several people said that they had been part of the collective euphoria surrounding the demonstrations to create an independent Armenia, but they had not really thought through the reality of governance, which requires experienced bureaucrats who are impartial, efficient, and honest. One person said that the transition from communism to democracy developed too quickly:

> I'm not as happy now [in contrast to under Soviet rule], simply because, I think, it was too fast. Things went too fast. I don't think we were ready for democracy. I don't think we really have democracy at this time. I know it will come eventually, after some time, when we learn more. But at this time, I think it's more chaotic. Many people ruined what's already there.

She added that capitalism was just an idea. People didn't really understand it. In her view, citizens needed to be educated regarding the ground rules of a capitalist, free-enterprise system. In her words, "How can you expect one to turn overnight into a capitalist?"

The more fundamental problem, however, was that some people felt that the country was in a virtual state of anarchy. One person said, "I always stood for my country, but now I can announce that there is anarchy in our country. There are no laws, no rules. . . . The new government is like no government. They neither lead, nor govern, nor control." Laws were not being enforced. Officials were taking bribes. And the mafia, according to some, was controlling some of the business activity, including the transportation of fuel and natural gas into the country. Some people even felt that the mafia might actually be blowing up the pipelines that brought gas to Armenia through Georgia so that they could profit from importing fuel. And some also felt that government officials were collaborating with the mafia.

The views on President Ter-Petrossian varied from complete support to strong criticism. The critiques of the president were typically highly pragmatic: he was failing to provide bread and heat, or to regenerate the economy. People faulted him for promising things that he could not deliver. "He put his hand on the Holy Bible, and look at him, one lie after another. Whatever he said, whatever he promised, has gone down the drain." On the other hand, some people strongly supported Ter-Petrossian, arguing that he was their elected official. One person succinctly said, "He is our leader. He is capable. He is our president. We strongly support him." This same person found the president's words comforting: "I respect our president, Levon Ter-Petrossian. The other day he talked, and he gave us hope. He said that Karabakh will soon end. That we don't have too many difficult days left. What he was trying to tell us was 'Be hopeful. These days will pass.'"

Others were realistic about their new government, claiming that the problems of Armenia were greater than any one person could solve. The dissolution of the Soviet Union had put all of the republics at risk because of the way the Soviet economy was structured:

> You see, the whole Soviet Union had sunk to a rather low level. Their stability had gone. They were on the verge of falling apart. So the end was here. No matter who took over, it would still have been hard. So let no political party tell me that if they had taken over they could have done better. With the blockade, with all the resources lacking, there was no way that the country could have done better.

Also, communism had put them at a decided disadvantage for implementing a viable democracy. "You see, for seventy years we were under communist reign. Under that kind of reign, leadership, how could we prepare leaders to govern us today?"

Nevertheless, some people saw virtues in the communist system. In particular, they admired the law, order, and discipline that characterized the Soviet Union. They also acknowledged that the Soviet Union as a whole had a collective power and influence, worldwide, that they could not hope to achieve as a small, independent republic. Also, almost no one disagreed that they were better off financially under Soviet rule. Still, a solid majority of the people we interviewed felt strongly that they did not wish to return to communism. To the question "Would you rather go back to communism?" one person said, "No, never. Under communism I think we were better off. I can say that. But I sure don't want that regime to return. No!" Another individual argued, however, that the communists were still involved in leadership. "No, I don't want communism to return. But what happened is that the former leaders are still in power, and bribery continues, and this is not good. I don't like it. We don't need them."

What some people acknowledged that they did need, however, was a strong alliance with Russia. As the smallest of the former Soviet republics, Armenia was vulnerable. The following statement was typical: "You see, Armenia cannot survive without the Russians. We have too many enemies. We are surrounded by enemies, and we alone cannot do it. We need the Russians to support us, to keep us from all our enemies." Another person stated the same point in different words: "Armenians cannot live alone. They need a big nation to support them." And another was even more emphatic: "Without the Russians, we are lost. We are totally dependent on Russia, and if we ever lose them, if they ever give us up, or we just give them up, we're lost." At the same time, some felt disgust at the lack of support from the Russians, especially regarding the events in Sumgait: "What was Sumgait for them? Why did they not prevent it? Was that something that they wanted to occur?"

In questioning the role of Russia, many people felt that Gorbachev was to blame for the disorderly transition to independence and democracy. Not only did he move slowly to quell the violence against Armenians in Azerbaijan, but he encouraged the various republics to pursue independence and then did not support them in making a viable economic transition to democracy. Responding to Gorbachev's initiatives, one person argued that the problem was not the ideal of independence but the timing associated with it:

> I believe that it was too early for independence, because, economically, Armenia wasn't prepared for such a step. The same can be said about all of the other fourteen republics. We were greatly connected with Russia. This is also a political issue. All of the republics were connected to each other economically, and they weren't able to exist separately from each other. That's why this separation was so painful.

Nevertheless, he said, "I want to believe that Armenia will rise again." At the same time, he acknowledged, "It's sad to realize that years will pass, and the quality of life will get worse." He did not see an easy resolution to Armenia's need to feed its population, educate them, and clothe them, but he said, "We live with hope."

The dilemma confronting democracy in the years after independence was that it failed to produce a better life, at least at a material level, than people had experienced under communism. We spoke with some people who appeared to be completely alienated from the political process. One person summed up his feelings about politics by saying, "I can say that I am bored with it because it is in such a state of chaos." An even stronger statement of disenchantment was issued by a widow now living alone:

> I have absolutely no faith, nor interest [in politics]. I don't approve of anything. Our condition is bad. I don't see any hope. I look at the past and wish that we had some stability, some food, which we have none or very little of. I totally disapprove of what is going on in Karabakh. I am disenchanted with the government, with how they manage, control. That's where I stand.

This sentiment, however, was not often stated so strongly. Most people wanted to give democracy a chance. Indeed, one person said that they could not just put the blame on their leaders. After all, they were elected by the people, he said.

A fairly large number of people knew that their political problems had to be seen in a geopolitical context, rather than in the narrow context of the relationships between Armenia, Turkey, and Azerbaijan. For example, they believed that the United States had its own interest in maintaining relationships with the Republic of Turkey because it is a neutral buffer between Western Europe and Russia. Likewise, Russia had an interest in Armenia because it is a Christian enclave in a region that is dominantly Muslim and is also an impediment to the union of Turkey and Azerbaijan as one front against Russia. They also recognized that Armenia's relationship with Iran was problematic because of U.S. opposition to Islamic fundamentalism in that country. The last hope, Armenia's neighbor to the north, Georgia, has been unreliable in its support of Armenia. Offering a somewhat fatalistic analysis, one person said, probably quite accurately, "Big countries have their own political interest, and they will do whatever comes first in their political interests, and they are not interested in little countries and their desires and their problems." The following are typical comments that were scattered throughout our interviews:

> It's true, the United States has been an ally of Turkey for the one reason that it is a safe place for them, a neutral ground against the Middle East, against Russia, against the enemy.

> Thus, you see, Russia is on our side because Russia does not want in any way for the Turks to bother us, because then they'll be in danger.

> If you want to establish some kind of trade with Iran, you have to go over a fairly mountainous region. It's not easy. The roads aren't in good shape. The weather conditions in the winter are so severe that it makes that fairly impossible without really good roads.

The bottom line, in the words of one person, is that "we don't have access to the sea." Summarizing their plight, another person said, "It is sad; our geographical location is so bad that we have no access to the outer world. We are surrounded by enemies." This landlocked status makes Armenia very vulnerable to the tactic of blockades as a form of political coercion. Their one hope to the north, Georgia, has proven to be an unfaithful partner.

> I understand Azerbaijan's actions, but I don't understand Georgia's. She is our only "Sister in Christ," but she plays dirty games with us. Even if a Georgian were listening to me now, I would still say that what they do is indecent for a Christian republic. I understand the Azeris: They are set against us because of the Karabakh conflict. But what's wrong with the Georgians? Now Georgians harm Armenia more than Azerbaijan does.

Such geopolitical analysis led one interviewee to conclude that the hands of Armenia's leaders were tied. Whatever they did, the political context was against them. If Armenia is to survive, however, it must negotiate political compromises with its neighbors that are acceptable on all sides. A refugee from Baku remarked realistically, "We won't disappear. Armenia will continue existing for centuries and so will Azerbaijan, Turkey, and others. Therefore, we have to learn how to live like neighbors if we want to live at all."

Solving the Energy Problem

The earthquake, the war, and the blockade were three major events that affected the welfare of people in Armenia, and the fourth was surely the decision to close the Medzamor nuclear power plant, because it did as much to suffocate Armenia's industry as did the blockade. Hindsight is always 20/20, but the great majority of people who commented on the closure of the plant felt that it was a terrible mistake. Clearly, the entire population was concerned about the safety of the generating plant in the wake of the disaster in Chernobyl and the devastating earthquake in Armenia, but it was also clear from our interviews that the implications of closing Medzamor had not been thought through clearly. Few people had considered what Armenia would do in the event of a blockade. No one had lined up alternative sources of energy within Armenia, such as geothermal generators, wind, or coal. Hence, closing the plant put Armenia in an extremely vulnerable position.

When our research assistant asked one woman whether she was originally for or against the closing of the nuclear station, she said, "I openly said nothing. We were scared after what had happened in Chernobyl." Consequently, she went along with what seemed to be the prudent thing to do if safety was the only issue. Others were even more pointed in expressing the emotions that surrounded the closure: "The story of Chernobyl is still fresh in our minds, the awful destruction that it caused to so many. To this day, thousands suffer physically because of it. So that's a threat to us today." Some people recognized that in a country as small as Armenia, a major disaster could have a devastating effect on the entire population—as well as their neighbors. However, the alternative to being without power was to return to the stone age. One person said that the lack of electricity has turned them into "cavemen." Hence, although they knew the dangers of operating the station, many people were willing to deal with the risk of an accident—simply because the alternative of not having power was equally bad, in their opinion. "Yes, I want it to open, because it will be our only source of energy, even though I am afraid about the dangers that it might present. I have been told that it could explode and kill the whole country."

A prevailing view was that the nuclear power station should have stayed open at least until alternative energy sources could be identified. Here is a typical comment: "It was a shortsighted action. First, they should have seen to it that we had enough energy, then they could have closed it. It was shortsighted and wrong."

Other people's view of the closure was colored by a general disaffection with the communist government that had stuck them with this unsafe technology, along with several other industries that were major polluters:

> How was it possible for a group of people to close down the three major economic giants of Armenia: the atomic station and the synthetic rubber and copper industries? Today, we see the results. I will never forget how the ex-chairman of the Council of Ministers, when giving a speech at a session of the Supreme Council, was very passionate about the station. He was saying—by the way, it was in Russian—"Dear Comrades, we shouldn't, shouldn't close the station down," but no one listened to him. He was believed to be from "the older generation"—one of Gorbachev's people— and, since he was from Stavropol, he was not considered a real Armenian.

Corresponding with this view was the opinion that people had reacted emotionally, politically, to the option of closing the plant and did not take appropriate counsel from the scientific community. An engineer said regarding the closure, "That was one of the most foolish things to do. It was a very tragic mistake. Most people who are being asked about this are not qualified to discuss it. Only people specializing in the field can talk about the consequences of such an action." Supporting the view that citizens responded emotionally to the possible danger of the reactor, someone said, "It was utterly wrong to close the nuclear plant. See, we are like sheep; worse than sheep. I think we are stupid [referring to following those who advocated closure]." In his opinion, the closure of the plant put Armenia a decade behind the economic advancement of neighboring countries, such as Azerbaijan.

Those who supported closure even after they had seen its consequences typically held out hope that Armenia had alternative energy resources in the form of oil or coal. There were also a few people who took a long-term view, suggesting that a network of smaller power-generating units could be constructed that would utilize a broad spectrum of energy sources, ranging from wind to solar, hydroelectric, and geothermal. Only one hardliner declared, "It's better for us to sit in darkness than be fearful lest there be an explosion. I don't trust the nuclear plant."

To Stay or Emigrate?

Lack of electricity was one of the main reasons that people decided to leave Armenia, because it created so many problems in their lives, from loss of employment to not being able to cook food or stay warm at night. When asked why she moved to Moscow, a physicist gave a long list of problems centered around trying to live a civilized life. While in Armenia her family lived on the tenth floor, and the elevator did not work; the water seldom reached to the level of their apartment; they had an electric stove, but very intermittent electricity to use it; the bread available from the government was so hard it could not be chewed; it was extremely difficult to transport their children to school. In her words, "You try to stay patient for a long time, but, at some point, you just can't take it any longer and decide to leave. You want hot water, bread, and heat during the winter. That's how I got to Moscow."

Throughout our interviews people expressed deep love for Armenia—the land, the water, the nation. For some people, leaving Armenia was unthinkable; it would be like killing a part of themselves. Others had sacrificed so much—their sons, their husbands—that to leave Armenia would be to deny the ideals for which their loved ones had died. Still others felt that they were too old to establish roots elsewhere; they might as well die in the land of their forefathers. And then, of course, many families simply could not afford to leave because of the transportation costs.

We also heard opposing arguments, however, with some consistency. Loyalty to one's nation encountered the competing moral claim of the welfare of one's children. Raising them in an environment where they had no future and had to live an uncivilized life, deprived of electricity, daily showers, and a warm bed at night, was unfair. Some of the younger people also talked about feeling stalemated in their situation. They could not afford to move out of their parents' house, marry, or establish an independent life. They felt their only choice was to leave the country to find work. And then there were those who recognized that Armenians were a diaspora people. Because of previous hardships, they were now spread all over the globe. For them to leave Armenia was an unfortunate pattern, but it did not mean that they were any less Armenian. This was the history of their people, constantly moving for survival.

The dominant reply to our question about leaving Armenia, however, concerned the consequences for children of remaining. In an interview with a highly educated couple from Baku who had moved to Armenia, the wife said,

> Of course, I would like for Armenia to recover. But when will this be possible? My children need to get an education and go to school. In the winter, they had to miss four months of school, and they came back home blue from cold. Even in March it's cold in the schools. We want a normal human life. We need a minimum. We want to be able to bathe normally, we want electricity in our house, and we want a normal education for our children.

One man said bluntly, "When it comes down to feeding your family, you have to be practical. . . . I had a good childhood, and I want my children to have a good childhood. A normal childhood. A happy childhood. That's why I've chosen to live here in Moscow." Another man, who was still residing in Armenia, echoed the same sentiment when asked whether he was considering leaving: "With great heartache I would leave. I would leave just for the sake of my boys, because there is no future for them here."

It was clear that leaving would be an emotional and moral struggle for most people. As one person said hesitatingly, "I am very embarrassed to admit this, but if I had an opportunity, I would leave." In his view, his talents as an engineer and scientist were not being utilized, and he saw little prospect for his sons to take advantage of their training in radio-physics. He said that the only functioning field in Armenia was commerce, buying and selling. He had higher ambitions for himself and his two children. Another person deeply regretted having passed up an invitation from relatives to emigrate to Los Angeles. Her husband wanted to go, but she had resisted:

> That was five years ago. Now life has deteriorated to the point where I feel guilty. I look back and I know that I was wrong. I was utterly wrong. I look at my kids and see no future for them here. They are both very bright. My daughter is in medical school, and my son is interested in dentistry. I look at them and I think these bright kids have no future here. I was utterly wrong to oppose my husband.

In contrast, a man said, "My two sisters have gone to the United States. Time and again they have invited me to join them, but I will not. I am convinced that I need to stay here. It is okay for others to go. I cannot blame them, but I will stay here. It has to do with one's philosophy, one's conviction. Life is more than food. Food cannot control our destiny." On the other hand, one man claimed that he was more Armenian because he had chosen to leave Armenia. He argued forcefully that living in Moscow didn't mean that he was "not a true Armenian or that [he was] denying [his] nationality or profession." He said, "You see, a true Armenian man and father is the one who supports his family and puts his family first in his life." Still others argued that geographical location was not what constituted an Armenian, but whether one preserved the language, religion, and culture of Armenia.

Those who had already moved from Armenia—for example, to Moscow, where we did interviewing—usually expressed the view that when things returned to "normal," they would return to their homeland: "And if people manage to make the nuclear plant work again, we will have the most important things: electricity and gas. And many Armenians will return, because no matter how much you enjoy being a guest somewhere, it's better to be back home. Home attracts everyone back, no matter how good or bad each person's situation is." Indeed, many people we interviewed had long-term plans to return to Armenia. The reality, however, is that, at least in the short term, very few of the people who left Armenia have returned, and more have left. Even though electricity is now available, the exodus from Armenia continues. A more profound and morally ambiguous problem is that men who left Armenia in order to send money back to their families have often formed relationships with other women, married, had new families, and no longer support their wives and children at home, who, along with the elderly, make up one of the most desperately poor population groups in Armenia.

Historical Comparisons

When people make major decisions about their lives, such as whether to relocate to another country, they inevitably frame the decision by considering what has happened in the past and what might happen in the future. No one in our sample of nearly three hundred interviewees thought that Armenia would disappear (for example, by being overrun by Turkey and/or Azerbaijan to form one Islamic state); they believed firmly that Armenians always endure, regardless of hardships. At the same time, however, many people pointed to the 1915 genocide, which resulted in the complete depopulation of Armenians from Eastern Turkey, and acknowledged that the Armenian population's existence was threatened.

One person who was born in Sumgait said that the genocide seemed to her like a fable—that is, until the pogroms against Armenians occurred in her own city in 1988. "But when it happened to us in Sumgait, and I was an eyewitness to the torture and atrocities that the Turks caused the Armenians, I said, 'Wow, this is true.'" A man from Baku echoed the same transformation in historical consciousness:

> I had read about Turks forcing Armenians to leave their own lands, making them starve on the way, and just killing them. Killing those who were too weak to walk, including little babies, their mothers, and older people. I was reading these books in horror, finding it difficult to believe that something like that could really take place and, of course, I would never have believed that something similar could take place in the Soviet Union, now. I couldn't believe that one person could torture another one in a country like this one. [But] what I had read about I saw myself in real life. I saw myself what Turks have done to innocent people.

Others said that what was currently happening to Armenians was nothing more than a repetition of the genocide. A woman from Nagorno-Karabakh said, "I don't see any change or any difference. What we saw, the atrocities of 1988, were very similar to what the Armenian people saw in 1915 at the hands of the Turks."

People referred to the genocide not only with regard to the events in 1988 in Sumgait but also with regard to the war in Nagorno-Karabakh. Another person put the repetition theme in less particularistic terms: "You see, what our great grandfathers went through, we are going through now. It is history repeating itself. Suffering then, suffering now. War then, war now. Death then, death now." No one, however, compared the genocide to the tragedy of the earthquake, which was viewed as a natural phenomenon (although some people had conspiratorial theories about the earthquake being caused by the Russians).

Given this historical consciousness, we must ask whether the overlay of the genocide on current events in Nagorno-Karabakh and the Republic of Armenia influenced the decision of people to emigrate. While no one cited this as the precise reason, arguing, for example, that Armenians did not stand a chance against "the Turks," we can imagine that latent fears existed among Armenians who felt they were in a hopeless situation and had better leave while they had the opportunity. The "never again" conviction associated with the genocide can obviously cut in two directions:

one alternative is to fight to the end, so that "never again" would a person submit to slaughter like a sacrificial lamb. The other option is that "never again" would a person remain in a position to be attacked—emigration to a more democratically ruled country being the surest way to avoid this possibility.

6

Concluding Reflections

The Meaning of Being Human

In the first decade of Armenia's independence, this small republic has experienced more challenges than some countries encounter in a century. In many ways its future hangs in the balance. As we write, both Turkey and Azerbaijan are trying to suffocate Armenia by continuing an economic boycott that precludes trade across their borders. More than half of Armenia's population is living in poverty, and a quarter of its people are barely surviving, including many elderly and single-parent households. One of the essential ingredients for survival, namely, hope for the future, is ebbing for large numbers of people, as suggested by the fact that a quarter to one-third of the population has emigrated. The emotional and physical wounds of war, pogroms, and the earthquake lie just under the surface for many people, sapping the reservoir of strength that otherwise might be used to deal with the monumental challenges facing the country.

We might be expected, in this final chapter, to outline a program for resolving Armenia's problems. We could offer a few generalizations, but they would ring as mere platitudes related to the economy, settling the conflict in Nagorno-Karabakh, and calling for the Armenian diaspora to renew its commitment to the homeland. Mapping such large-scale so-lutions to intractable problems is a task for others: political scientists, economists, and state department officials. Instead, we have set ourselves a modest agenda for this chapter, one more fitting for the humanist than the policymaker. We want to share some reflections about the human sit-uation, those commitments that make us fundamentally human, and the potential to survive under difficult circumstances. The experience of the Armenian people holds lessons for us—insights garnered from our in-terviews that transcend Armenia's unique political situation and its strug-gle for survival.

The Human Situation

The earthquake in Armenia is a vivid reminder of our vulnerability as human beings. We are not omnipotent. We sometimes cannot control our destiny; our bodies are often subject to forces outside of ourselves. Earth-quakes, floods, fires, and other natural disasters take us off of our pedestal, revealing our dependency and inadequacy. Our ancestors sought to control these forces of nature by identifying them with gods who could be petitioned and perhaps influenced through sacrifices and prayers. Today we attempt to ameliorate the superior power of nature through stringent engineering standards, well-equipped fire departments, and disaster-preparedness plans. Nothing, however, can give us complete control over nature.

December 7, 1988, will forever stand as a memorial to nature's power—its potential for violence. Several images from our interviews stay with us. For example, the sea of grave markers in the Spitak cemetery, etched with images of children carrying their school bags, is a picture that is fixed indelibly in our minds. We expect to bury our elderly, but the tragedy of children snuffed out in the prime of their lives is something to which one can never be reconciled. Likewise, we cannot forget the mother who watched as rescuers unearthed her daughter, first an arm and then her entire body. This is the mother who said that she hoped her daughter would die with her, because she could not see how, given her current handi-capped status, this young woman could survive without her. Nor can we forget our conversation with the school principal who survived by tak-ing refuge under his desk as his school came crashing down, killing a dozen teachers and many times that number of students. And we are haunted by the faces of the teachers that we visited a decade later in the environs outside of Spitak. We looked in vain for a smile, a laugh, an acknowledgment of life's joys and pleasures.

As terrible as the earthquake was, we are even more troubled by the pogroms against Armenians in Azerbaijan. We do not want to believe that human beings can brutally attack, bludgeon, and burn the bodies of innocent people. But as the earth's crust is sometimes disrupted by forces deep within our planet, the thin veneer of civilization is equally subject to fracture by the base impulses latent in each of us. How could people randomly enter homes, throw their inhabitants off balconies, and beat them senseless with their own household implements? What is the source of the evil that would compel people to strip naked a pregnant woman, burn her body with cigarettes, and then light her on fire with kerosene? How could fellow citizens watch these atrocities without being so outraged that the perpetrators would be massively repelled?

Such events are not unique to Azerbaijan, however, and we need to go beyond local problems to seek deeper explanations of the source of violence among human beings. The pogroms against Armenians are only one example of the human capacity for evil. We only need to look at the public lynchings of African Americans to see other examples, or the murder of Jews and Gypsies during the Second World War, or, more recently, the genocides in Cambodia and Rwanda. While theologians offer theories of the fall from innocence, what we know pragmatically is that civilized behavior is no accident. It is the product of political institutions that hold in check our capacity for violence. In the case of the pogroms against Armenians, clearly the Russian military failed to prevent anarchy from developing within a political climate that encouraged violence against a minority population. If there is a lesson to be taken from these events, it is the universal mandate to never be a bystander, to intervene, even at the risk of one's own life, in order to protect the life and dignity of other persons.

The war in Nagorno-Karabakh also holds deep insights into human nature. It reminds us that we are fundamentally communal beings whose identity rests as much on our collective claims as on our individual achievements. The Armenians of Karabakh frequently referred to the land as the soul of their people—it was sacred and worth dying for. To lose the war would have been to lose an important element of their own being. Only this framing of the issue can explain the tenacity with which Armenians fought for their independence and the huge costs they were willing to pay in terms of their comfort, well-being, and personal sacrifice of loved ones to the war effort.

If we ignore the collective rationale for war and focus only on personal tragedy, then war is an utterly nonsensical activity. When we visited the hotel in Stepanakert where hundreds of refugee families were living, we were repeatedly struck by the terrible consequences of war—especially when we saw the photographs of fathers and husbands who had been killed that were pinned to the walls. This tragedy was reaffirmed when young boys of eight or twelve told our interviewers how they missed their dads and that, if they could have anything in this world, it would be the return of their fathers to the family. At the same time, one must hold in the balance the statements of refugee women who said that they would return to their land as soon as it was safe, even if they had to rebuild everything from the ground up. Their personal meaning was connected with the soil of their birthplace. We can see, therefore, that it is part of the human condition for personal meaning to be intimately tied to a collective identity that is rooted in geography.

Hence, while we have attempted to present an oral history account of major events in the lives of Armenians in the post-Soviet era, these events serve as a microcosm for a much broader examination of the human condition. The earthquake mirrors our finitude as human beings; the pogroms in Azerbaijan reveal the need to moderate the baser human instincts through authority backed by power; and the war clearly shows that purely individualistic analyses of human nature are inadequate. We are communal beings, tribal creatures, who find meaning in our collective identifications.

The fourth major focus of our research, of course, was on the painful effects of the blockade as dramatized in the suffering brought on by winter conditions, hunger, and massive unemployment. In many ways this situation simply reflects the human tendency toward group identification. It is the age-old competition of "us" against "them"—of the Turks against the Armenians, although we could substitute different nationalities or tribal affiliations for the historic domination of Turks over Armenians. Thus, the very thing that gives individuals roots, a sense of heritage, a set of collective values, and therefore a bulwark of communal support is also the occasion for group conflict and great human tragedy. This paradox, unfortunately, is the human condition.

The Fundamentally Human

Much of this book is filled with accounts of violence and human suffering, but these descriptions are not what touched our conscience. What affected us at a deeply personal level were attempts to confront violence and personal loss and people's efforts to offer comfort, love, and assistance to others in need. Violence, greed, death, and self-interest are somehow endemic to the human condition, but attempts to overcome or cope with these baser elements of life reveal our deepest humanity. We could cite many illustrations of this humanity from our interviews, but let us recall just a few that caused us to pause for a moment and think about what is fundamentally human.

We find ourselves thinking often about the child in Spitak who was sitting all alone at night after the earthquake, holding a stick with a picture of his father, illuminated by a single candle. This child's effort to make a vigil for his dead father is a quintessentially human act. Rituals, even of the simplest sort, are attempts to mediate and express what is most sacred to us. In the same vein, we think of the young child who was taking food to the cemetery to feed his deceased family members. However naive this act may appear to adult eyes, it was an expression of care, an effort to maintain a connection with those whom he loved.

Such stories speak to the very deepest qualities of our humanity, namely, that what matters most are relationships with loved ones. But we were also touched to see people reaching out to complete strangers. We encountered children in the subway begging, such as the boy who was singing for donations, hoping that someone would acknowledge his humanity. We heard that during the flight from the front lines of the war in Nagorno-Karabakh, when refugees encountered mothers and infants who were alone and without any means of sustenance, they stopped and helped them, offering them food or money.

We also admire the many Azerbaijanis who sheltered Armenians in danger during the pogroms in 1988–90. Armenians by the hundreds were taken into the homes of Azeris who rejected the scapegoating of their neighbors. Likewise, we acknowledge the humanity of those Azerbaijanis who later apologized to Armenians for the acts committed by their countrymen against them. Such attempts to heal the moral breach between two groups of people—people separated only by the accident of their birthright—point to the most profound elements of our humanity.

Gift-giving is also a quintessentially human act. Many people survived the deadly winters after independence because friends and relatives assisted them. Sometimes a gift of food came from a brother or sister-in-law who farmed in a village outside of Yerevan. Or a financial gift might have come from abroad, even from people of extremely modest means.

More typically, people gave a few cups of flour to make bread, or shared firewood with those who could not gather their own. And of course we must note the generous gifts that came from foundations, governments, and large philanthropic organizations.

Surviving with Dignity

When we try to think of the elements that distinguish people who survived with dignity from those who were marked by despair, several concrete examples immediately come to mind. On the negative front, there were people who isolated themselves from others. Because they could not entertain friends by offering them food and sending them away with gifts—which is the Armenian custom—they simply quit socializing. Other people were afraid to be seen in public because of their threadbare clothes, so they avoided public settings. On the other hand, there were people who banded together with neighbors and relatives, meeting in each other's homes to share the warmth of a stove and to commiserate, as well as to tell stories and play games. One couple, for example, saw the long evenings as a time to sing, dusting off instruments that otherwise were seldom used. And a child said that during the winter he got to know his parents and siblings in a way that he had not previously because they spent hours talking together. In short, human community became a form of compensation for the physical deprivation that people were experiencing. To some degree, Americans discovered this same basis for their humanity after the September 11 terrorist bombings in the United States.

Maintaining hope was the intangible factor that kept people alive. Unfortunately, however, some people simply gave up and turned inward, attending only to the most basic bodily functions. Perhaps this is inevitable for some, but others were able to frame their lives and future in ways that enabled them to surmount their immediate survival needs. We were struck by how many times women said that their children gave them hope. Somehow looking into their eyes each morning motivated these mothers to push ahead. We were also impressed by the way children, perhaps in their innocence, refused to give up and in some cases even ended up comforting their parents.

Many people also turned to religion as a source of comfort. They spoke of going to church to light a candle in memory of someone they had lost, seeking solace in a strength that was greater than their own. And many priests, especially in the earthquake zone, practiced the ancient art of putting an arm around someone and offering them comfort. Human touch is a powerful mediator of the divine that is within each of us.

Concluding Thoughts

For diaspora Armenians reading this book, our hope is that the connection with their roots will be reawakened—or at least reaffirmed. There is something very sad and tragic about the history of the Armenian people. It is reflected in their songs, poetry, and other artistic productions. But this is not the time to become absorbed in the "good life" that many have found outside the motherland, forgetting their kinsmen in the Republic of Armenia. The diaspora is a rich resource for the people of the Republic of Armenia. However, an important qualification is in order. A new type of charity, a new philanthropy, is required from diaspora Armenians. Direct aid is sometimes appropriate, especially in caring for the elderly and for children. The most urgent need, however, is for new forms of partnership that will create jobs, rebuild the economic infrastructure of the country, and nurture responsible democratic institutions. A message that we heard repeatedly in our interviews is that Armenians do not want to be dependent; they do not want to be pitied. Instead, they want to stand on their own, establish their own businesses, and create a viable economy.

This desire for self-sufficiency is laudable and obviously is the foundation for building a new economy. It opens the door to many kinds of small businesses in which true partnerships can be created. Furthermore, it is important for outside government aid to focus on building a new economy in Armenia, because the old economy could only work within the structure of the Soviet system. Even such programs as child sponsorship should seek to do more than feed and clothe children. These youth must learn skills and develop leadership abilities that will enable them to support their families in the future. And economic structures must be developed that will enable them to be productive citizens.

When we were traveling with the photographic exhibit that was created in concert with this project, the most enthusiastic audience was inevitably young professionals who felt a genuine moral burden to connect with their homeland, and they frequently asked us what they should do. For second- and third-generation Armenians who have never been to Armenia, our advice was to visit and establish relationships with people from their homeland. People living in the Republic of Armenia need to feel that they have not been forgotten by the world community. Outsiders, if not patronizing, can mediate hope, and in the process they may find a niche that connects their skills and resources with an institution or group of individuals within Armenia.

For non-Armenians, the Republic of Armenia is a case study in the plight of at least a billion people on our globe. Armenia's situation is unique, but aspects of it echo through the stories of other nations, including Kosovo, other republics in the former Soviet Union, and many African countries—including Rwanda, where we are currently developing an oral history project with surviving orphans. In this regard, Armenia is a paradigm that deserves study because of what it reveals about independence struggles, human nature, and geopolitics. If we can moralize for a moment, we believe that every American should have a significant connection with a developing country that involves both intimate knowledge of the setting and some form of personal partnership.

Recently we spent several evenings looking slowly through the pages of a magnificent book of photographs by Sebastião Salgado called *Migrations*. These pictures reminded us of the stories from our interviews in Armenia, because statistics were turned into faces the faces of individuals who are struggling to find dignity in a world that threatens their humanity. It is easy to remain detached from generalizations about poverty, genocide, and natural disaster. It is not so easy to ignore the eyes of someone in need. These pictures visually and viscerally make the point that we have no control over the place and time of our birth, and if we happen to live a privileged life, then we have corresponding obligations to share our resources.

While labeling people is a way of maintaining our sanity—especially when we blame them for their situation—great human richness arises from being sensitive to the plight of others, experiencing a bit of their pain, and identifying with their hope for a better life. We hope that this book has mediated this experience for you. Personally, we will not be quite the same as a result of listening to the three hundred people who volunteered their stories, and so we wish to thank them for sharing a moment of their lives with us. In particular, we have been given a new appreciation for some of the most elementary things of everyday life, including food, running water, heat, and employment. We have also been reminded that people often die for very fundamental values—independence, freedom, and the right of self-governance—so that they can pass them on to others.

Epilogue

Ten Years after Independence

In the spring of 2001 we decided to return to Armenia with the explicit goal of assessing how things had changed since our research in 1993 and 1994. Several events made this a propitious moment for our visit: First, it was nearly ten years since Armenia had declared independence from the former Soviet Union; second, we would be there on April 24, the eighty-sixth anniversary of the Armenian genocide; and, third, this was the 1,700th anniversary of Armenia's embrace of Christianity, and a new cathedral was being completed in Yerevan. In addition, there was a personal element connected with this trip. Fifteen of Lorna's family members would be visiting Armenia, including our daughter, several of her cousins, and five of Lorna's siblings and their spouses. This trip had been dreamed up at the family's annual Thanksgiving dinner, and to everyone's disbelief, all members of the group had honored their commitment.

We converged in London for a happy, multigenerational gathering. One sister and brother-in-law had traveled dozens of times to Armenia, representing a group of San Francisco Armenians who were supporting schools in Armenia, as well as soup kitchens and various medical projects.

Lorna's eldest brother had also traveled numerous times to Armenia, working with scientists on energy-related research. The great unknown about this trip, however, was the response of the half-Armenian cousins, eager to explore their identity but uncertain of what awaited them as they set foot on the enigmatic soil of their motherland.

From Heathrow Airport we took off in a sleek, new British Airways jet. Armenia Airlines now had competition. En route we sat next to a specialist on international deforestation. He was clearly discouraged with the progress Armenia was making since the tree-cutting period of the early 1990s. He lamented that an important government post had recently been given to a baker who had no expertise in forest management. We asked if this was the result of the brain-drain that had occurred, or had the post been purchased for a price? He did not know, but worried that either way the outcome would be the same. On the other hand, we met a woman on the plane from a U.S.-based NGO that was planting trees in Armenia. She clearly loved her mission in life, stating it was the most upbeat thing she had ever done. In some ways, these two people were symbolic of what we were to find during much of our trip. Structurally, Armenia was in terrible shape, but one could always find good hearted people who were attempting to make a difference.

We landed in Yerevan at the Zvartnots International Airport. The luggage arrived within minutes on a conveyor belt. We breezed through customs. Our bus was waiting at the curb to take us, along with the Touryan clan, to a hotel in Yerevan. The only hassle was from a group of men who were overly eager to carry our luggage. What a contrast to our first visit, in 1990! On that trip we had landed in the dark and had been herded into a small room where we waited endlessly for our luggage—only to have it dumped in a pile through which everyone scrabbled to locate their possessions—and then waited in a disorganized queue to exit through a tiny doorway manned by a single airport official.

We could no longer afford the Hotel Armenia, where we had previously stayed. Even a simple room was well over a hundred dollars a night, so we had booked rooms a few hundred yards away at the Erebuni Hotel, which was reasonable at $60 a night, and that price included a living room suite along with breakfast in a Soviet-style dining room that was intended to impress with its size and grandeur. The breakfast was plentiful: coffee, tea, hard- and soft-boiled eggs, fig jam, sliced meats, potato-filled pancakes. What more could one ask for? There was even a bar on the ground floor.

Although we had visited Armenia in 1998, it was still a shock to walk up Abovian Street from Republic Square and encounter boutiques with the latest women's fashions, upscale pizza restaurants, outdoor cafés, and a new hotel in which any head of state or corporate CEO would feel at home. Our memories of Abovian Street from the early 1990s were of stores with nothing on their shelves, one or two outdoor cafés that served coffee in cracked cups, and cars coasting downhill with their engines off as their drivers tried to save gasoline. Yes, things had changed. Lines of taxis waited for fares. The fountains in Republic Square were flowing. Clearly some people were living a decent life. That first evening we headed to the National Opera House, passing through the same square where hundreds of thousands of people had gathered a decade ago to demonstrate for the liberation of Nagorno-Karabakh and for their own independence. Now the square was populated with cafés and round tables with colorful umbrellas. The tulips were in full bloom. Music was playing over loudspeakers. Couples were strolling arm in arm. One could have easily mistaken this scene for a piazza in Italy.

It may not have been the Bolshoi Ballet, but the dancing that night by the National Dance Ensemble evoked the emotion that only a local troupe of Armenians could have inspired as they commemorated the upcoming anniversary of the 1915 genocide. Tears flowed down our cheeks. Whatever the state of the Armenian economy, the arts were once again vibrant. Several times during our stay we went back to the Opera House—once to hear the Armenian Symphony Orchestra play a Shostakovich violin concerto, and on another occasion to hear several outstanding vocalists sing the arrangements of Armenian composers. Music was also bubbling up from the grassroots. We were surprised one Sunday to hear a nine-year-old violinist give a virtuoso performance as part of a worship service, and on another occasion we met a teenage pianist who had just cut her first CD.

Because Lorna's extended family was on this trip, we also visited some of the historic churches and monuments of Armenia. In addition to three beautiful twelfth-century churches near Dilijan, we went to Geghard Monastery, a spectacular church carved into the side of a mountain. In this cavelike church one of Lorna's sisters began singing the Lord's Prayer, and everyone joined in, except for the cousins who had lost their mother tongue. Their role was to wipe away the tears that welled up in their eyes as the ancient voice of their tradition awakened something deep within their spirits. There were many times of celebration in these several weeks of travel. Every lunch hour a long table was set, and amid the raised brandy glasses and toasts, the shish kebab, trout from Lake Sevan, *pilav,* and tomatoes, we discussed the future of Armenia, the role of the diaspora, and how this trip was changing each person's perception of the world.

Early one morning we walked ten minutes from our hotel to the new cathedral that was being built to commemorate Armenia's 1,700 years as a Christian nation. Climbing through the construction debris, we entered this nearly completed structure, which was ten times the size of many of Armenia's historic churches. As we looked upward at the huge dome, we remembered an Armenian entrepreneur we had met in Bangkok, home to no more than fifty Armenians, who had given generously to support this monument to the spirit of the Armenian people and their Christian faith. We also remembered a church we had visited in Ravenna, Italy, that carried in its dome and mosaics the marks of an Armenian architect and craftsmen. Echoing through our thoughts was the memory that Armenians are a diaspora people: more than half of them live outside the Republic of Armenia.

Even though language and religion are the two fundamental sources of Armenian identity, when the Republic of Armenia became independent in 1991, Christianity was rather moribund. The institution existed, but the soul had been sucked out of the people. The god of communism was the state. Religion was an opiate that retarded social progress, according to Marxist theory. The fall of communism, however, created an ideological vacuum throughout the former Soviet Union, including the Republic of Armenia. After a few glitches in church-state relations (particularly in the mid-1990s), there is now relative freedom of religion in Armenia. The ranks of men studying in seminaries of the Apostolic Church have swelled. There is also a vigorous Protestant movement, although it represents only a small percentage of the population. It includes a Pentecostal church that we visited, whose membership has grown to several thousand young adults in a decade.

Amid all the difficulties that beset the Armenian people, they are experiencing a spiritual renaissance. One morning we had breakfast with someone who had lived for years in Armenia working for various NGOs, who linked economic renewal with spiritual revitalization. He had not given up on business-related renewal projects within the country. He had noticed both a shift in the way businesses responded to their consumers and a change in the way business owners treated their employees— shedding some aspects of the authoritarian Soviet management style. While musing about the entrepreneurial spirit of Armenians, however, he wondered if there was not a corresponding need for a spiritual transformation within the country—that is, a moral renewal that would provide the basis for more transparent accounting practices, as well as integrity within government and law enforcement. Echoing his views, nearly everyone we asked said that corruption was a major problem in this fledgling democracy, and that the future of the country depended on eradicating this legacy from communism.

Early in our visit we went to the office of the World Bank to get the latest publication on the economy ("Republic of Armenia: Interim Poverty Reduction Strategy Paper," March 2001). There was some good news, but the report also expressed a lot of pain. From 1994 (the year our interviews ended) to 2000, annual real gross domestic product (GDP) growth averaged 5.4 percent, and per capita income increased from US$173 to US$503. Unfortunately, however, per capita income in the year 2000 was one-third what it was in 1990, prior to independence, when the average income was US$1,590. Economically, it has been a rough ride. Industrial output plummeted 54 percent from 1991 to 1993, largely because of the collapse of regional trade and the difficulties of replacing a central planning system with a market economy. In 2000, the average household's purchasing power was nine times lower than in 1990, placing about two-thirds of the population at or below the poverty level, with roughly a quarter of the population ranked as extremely poor.

This same World Bank report gives a very poor report card to education in Armenia. Teachers are earning US$10–$20 a month, and a lag time of several months often occurs between payments. Such conditions have encouraged teachers to tie student grades to bribes—for example, requiring parents to pay teachers for special tutoring of their children. Basic educational materials, including textbooks, paper, and pencils, are at a premium. Heating schools during the winter is still a problem. And basic maintenance in the schools is deplorable.

The report also indicates that health care is unaffordable for most Armenians. The government spends only 1.6 percent of GDP on health, creating a situation in which 90 percent of patients are forced to make "informal" payments to doctors and health-care workers if they are to get adequate service. Health-care institutions receive between one half and one third as many visits as they did in 1990. In addition, both pregnancy rates and marriage rates have declined precipitously. Many elderly people forgo medication in favor of bread.

A study copublished in 1998 by the government of Armenia, UNICEF, and Save the Children offered an equally bleak picture ("A Situation Analysis of Children and Women in Armenia"). This report tells the same story as the World Bank study. In the 1970s and 1980s, industrial production accounted for more than two-thirds of Armenia's GDP. The earthquake wiped out 40 percent of the republic's production capacity. The collapse of the Soviet Union exacerbated the problems of access to raw goods and markets, and by 1997 the output of the industrial sector had shrunk to 29 percent of GDP. The rate of real unemployment in 1998 was estimated at 32 percent, even though the government's official figure was one-third that rate.

Given these conditions, how are people surviving? A major part of the answer to this question lies in the fact that 35 percent of household income in 1997 was coming from "private transfers" (i.e., from family members and relatives living abroad). Without this income supplement, many Armenians would be desperately poor. In this regard, families in the Republic of Armenia parallel those in Mexico and Central America, who often rely heavily on remittances from relatives living in the United States. For Armenians, however, many of these family members are living in Russia, where incomes are modest at best.

In some ways these statistics did not jibe with the revitalized economy that we were witnessing in the area around our hotel in Yerevan. So we went in search of other evidence. Quite by accident, we ran across one of our former research assistants. He was making a relatively reasonable income working for a Swiss-based NGO, but he sadly reported that what we saw in central Yerevan was a bubble of affluence. In his view, less than 10 percent of the population of the city could afford to eat or shop in the district surrounding our hotel and the Opera Square. He confirmed that 70 percent of the population is making less that $50 per month. He also stated his conviction that the only hope for Armenia is a new generation of youth who will understand capitalism rather than simply mimic it. Like many other people we encountered, he was distressed over the corruption he saw around him, and he reiterated what our previous breakfast companion had said, namely, that a moral and spiritual transformation is necessary if the old system of bribes and under-the-table dealing is to be replaced with transparent financial transactions.

While many people had reaffirmed the poverty of large segments of the Armenian population, we had spent the first week of our visit in a rather restricted orbit of commercial affluence. So one day we decided to visit some of the soup kitchens that were being supported by American donations. They were filled with children and the elderly. The noon meal being offered was substantial, with extra food being taken home in jars for other family members. The kids were bright-eyed and happy;

the mothers, however, looked worn and depressed. The organizers of this kitchen said that many more soup kitchens were needed, but they had decided to maintain the quality of the food rather than water it down in order to serve more people. Unfortunately, it seems that "compassion fatigue" has set in: the budget of this organization has remained nearly constant for the past few years, in spite of aggressive fund-raising.

Next on our list was a woman representing a relief organization that supplies food directly to families on a monthly basis. The biggest change since 1994, she said, is that fathers who have gone abroad to work are forming new families in Russia and elsewhere, leaving their children and wives back in Armenia without any means of support. She also said that, since our last visit in 1998, people seem to be losing hope; they cannot see any resolution to their poverty. The ecstasy of the liberation struggle has long since worn off.

We heard an equally bleak story from a nun (non-Armenian) who had dedicated her life to serving children in Lebanon and now, in retirement— if one could call it that—was serving elderly Armenians, many of whom have been left behind by their children who have gone abroad. She said that government retirement payments to the elderly cannot possibly sustain them, which explains why we were seeing elderly people begging on the streets—an almost unheard-of phenomenon in Armenian culture. Furthermore, any savings they might have accumulated have been destroyed by inflation. This nun said that very few elderly people, in her opinion, have adequate health care. They simply cannot afford medication or doctor's visits.

Later in our trip we visited one of the homes for the elderly in Gyumri. Some of the rooms had been renovated by the charitable giving of Armenians in the United States, but the rest of the building was really dismal. The plaster on the walls was cracked, and the paint was peeling. It was obvious that the heating system was barely functional. After several hours of visiting with residents, we left with truly ambivalent feelings. On one hand, the humanity and generous spirit of the people living there is remarkable; furthermore, the ability to create a clean, stimulating place for people to live in has been demonstrated. But, on the other hand, it is depressing to imagine one's own parents living out their days in the non-renovated section of the compound.

The next day, however, our spirits were buoyed once again. We interviewed Armenie Hovannisian, the wife of a former foreign minister of the Republic of Armenia. She told us how the Junior Achievement program in Armenia, which she directs, is providing textbooks and in-

structional materials to schools that model democratic debate and dis-
cussion of issues. Public figures, she said, are glad to meet with students
to discuss political issues in open forums. She and her husband, Raffi,
have also set up an after-school program for kids in Yerevan who are
wandering the streets in the afternoons and evenings. The formula for
starting this program was simple. This couple saw a need, looked at their
personal budget to see what they could afford, rented a facility where
youth could gather, and established a model program that now is at-
tracting private contributions.

This was not the only bright spot we encountered. Although many
educational institutions were in miserable condition, we visited schools
that were true beacons of hope. In the earthquake zone of Gyumri, for
example, we spent the morning in a new nursery school. Even though
many of the children came from very poor families, they were neatly
dressed. The children flashed smiles at us and clearly were motivated
learners, and they sang with a gusto that would be hard to top anywhere
in the world. Nearby we visited an older primary school that was equally
vibrant. The children were so engaged in learning that encompassed the arts
as well as the traditional reading, writing, and arithmetic. Not surpris-
ingly, both of these schools are receiving significant financial assistance
from abroad.

During the last week of our visit we traveled to Nagorno-Karabakh.
It was a spectacularly clear and beautiful day as we left Yerevan. Mount
Ararat was standing tall as usual, with only a few wispy clouds in the
sky covering its peak. On the way to Goris we stopped along a scenic
stream to have lunch. A clever family had diverted the water so that they
had their own little pool, where they were raising trout. We put in our
order for one each, and they were shortly dip-netted out, gutted, covered with salt, and put on sticks that were lowered down into a white-
hot *tonir* (a sunken oven), where they baked. In the meantime, we drank
a few toasts while we sat on a table next to the stream, feasting on cu-
cumbers, olives, and various herbs that were fresh from their nearby gar-
den. "Life is good," we confessed to each other before finishing off the
meal with a round of coffee served in demitasses.

When we hit the Lachin Corridor, the road was paved and marked with
American-style guardrails and signs—quite a contrast to the pothole-
marked road we had traveled seven years ago. Indeed, it was American-
raised money that surfaced this vital link between the Republic of Armenia and Nagorno-Karabakh. As we headed down the final grade into
Stepanakert, we pulled into a modernized gas station to meet the family

with whom we would stay for the next few nights. This could have been Switzerland, or the mountains of Southern California, for that matter. We were amazed at the scene. In 1993 there were literally no cars on the highway, and now we were waiting in a first-class gas station for our host, who showed up in a Russian-built luxury car. He took us to the three-story home that he had bought for $500 during the war, when the previous owner was fleeing for safety and the Azeris were a mere 20 kilometers from the city.

That afternoon we took a tour of Stepanakert. At one point we peeked around the corner of a new church that was being built and into the neighbor's yard. We saw people digging a large hole and asked what they were doing. The answer was obvious once it was stated: they were building a swimming pool! Well, why not? The war was over. The summer is hot. Life goes on, and why not enjoy a swim in the afternoon? This experience helped us adjust to the fact that there was also night life in Stepanakert, which was quite different from the ghost town that we had visited in 1993. That evening, after ice cream and coffee, we walked around the central square. The main government office had glass in the windows, rather than plastic. The hotel that had been filled with refugees now was open to tourists.

The next day we had a long talk with our host about his experiences during the past decade. He had personally buried 150 soldiers during the war. As if it were yesterday, he remembered the liberation struggle and the fact that he and his comrades knelt around their mortar launcher before firing it for the first time, praying: "You know our hearts; you know this mortar shell may kill innocent people. Save the innocent if this thing lands on the enemy side." He stressed that this war had been an act of self-defense, and that he and his family had fled to the capital city from Martakert along with fifty thousand other Armenians. When we asked him to compare the current situation in Nagorno-Karabakh with that in the Republic of Armenia, he said that people were returning to Nagorno-Karabakh, whereas they were still leaving Armenia. The people of Nagorno-Karabakh had an indomitable spirit, he said. They were rebuilding, resettling, and simultaneously protecting their borders. Too many lives had been lost to quit now.

On the last evening before heading home, Lorna's entire family clan crowded into our hotel bedroom suite, and each one spoke of his or her experience of the past few weeks. Without doubt, the younger generation had undergone the most profound transformations. One of the cousins said she was considering putting her legal career on hold in order to move to Armenia to become a teacher. Another cousin reflected on the possibility of shifting the emphasis of her doctoral dissertation to a focus on Armenia. They had all been shaken by their visit to a school for disabled children, where they had witnessed the heroism of the director—who was scraping together the money to care for several hundred children—and they were also deeply moved by seeing that many of these children were sleeping on cots in the hallways. They wondered how they could return to their affluent lifestyles in the United States without staying connected to these kids whose Armenian eyes looked so much like their own.

The twelfth-century churches they visited had also made a profound impression on them. Never again could they think of themselves in purely individualistic terms. They were part of a tradition, a heritage, to which they owed their very existence. Several of the cousins talked about the experience of walking up the road to the dungeon where St. Gregory the Illuminator had been held captive for so many years, with Mount Ararat towering in the background. There they had felt the blood call, a connection with their Christian heritage and the soil of Armenia.

In the closing minutes of our sharing, these cousins also expressed another feeling they had had while in Gyumri, when we had all stood around a large, rectangular table and raised our glasses after lunch in a toast to Medz Mama and Hairig—the parents and grandparents of this clan—both of whom were survivors of the 1915 genocide. Everyone had felt their presence, mystical yet real. It was as if this family had come home to its spiritual birthplace, to the land of its ancestral spirits. They had made this pilgrimage to the cradle of civilization to find themselves, and at the same time to leave a bit of themselves in the motherland. The next day as we all boarded the British Airways jet to London there was a strange silence. When would we return? What should our responsibility be, both Armenian and non-Armenian, to this tiny country whose survival is once again hanging in the balance? One thing was certain for all of us, however: Life outside of community has little meaning, and community carries with it a whole web of commitments—some distant and some more immediate—as we seek to create a more equitable world.

Appendix 1

Research Methodology

Although logistically much more complex, the research for this project parallels the methodology used for our book *Survivors: An Oral History of the Armenian Genocide* (University of California Press, 1993). The focus was on asking individuals to tell the story of their experiences regarding a particular set of events. We used a lengthy interview guide (see appendix 2) as a reference point for the interviewers, but it was not intended to structure the narrative account offered by the interviewees. Instead, we asked follow-up questions from the interview guide to probe issues that were not fully addressed in the story told by the interviewee. We never asked a single interviewee to answer all the questions on the interview guide. Rather, each interview focused on one of four specific topic areas: (1) the experience of the 1988 earthquake (e.g., loss of family members, destruction of homes, schools, sites of employment), plus attempts to rescue survivors as well as bury the dead; (2) the pogroms against Armenians living in Azerbaijan and the attempts of these refugees to settle in Armenia; (3) the experience of the war in Nagorno-Karabakh, including accounts by widows whose husbands had been killed and the flight of family members from the battlefront; and (4) problems surrounding surviving the winter because of the blockade imposed by Turkey and Azerbaijan against Armenia.

A total of 310 individual interviews were conducted with adults, Marineh Fstkchyan had 17 informal conversations with children in her school (many of whom were from refugee families), and our research team conducted two focus groups (one with teachers and another with benzine traders who were transporting fuel into Armenia). Fifty-five percent of the adult interviewees were women, and 45 percent were men. The average adult interviewed was forty-three years of age. Interviews averaged sixty-six minutes in length, and all interviews were tape-recorded on audiocassette tapes (excluding the conversations with children). Eighty-three percent of the interviews were conducted in Armenian, 15 percent were conducted in Russian (primarily the refugees from Azerbaijan who did not speak Armenian fluently), and five of the interviews (which included those of several people from NGOs) were conducted in English. While this was a snowball sample, interviewees were reasonably diverse, representing various educational levels and backgrounds. Of the 277 who offered employment information, 53 percent claimed to be employed full-time (which did not mean, of course, that they were being paid on a regular basis), 27 percent were unemployed, 15 percent were retired, 4 percent were working part-time, and 1 percent were receiving pensions. Of the 208 who provided marital status history, 40 percent were married, 32 percent were single, 22 percent were widowed, and 6 percent were divorced.

On our first trip to Armenia to initiate this project, we interviewed as potential interviewers a number of graduate students who had recently completed their TOEFL examination in English. We hired eight of these students (one man and seven women), along with Taline Satamian, a recent UCLA graduate who was working for *AIM* magazine as its Yerevan correspondent, and Korioun Alavardian, who had done extensive logistical planning for World Vision, an NGO working in the region. Taline Satamian served as a project consultant and listened to a number of the interviews before they were transcribed, regularly providing us with feedback regarding the quality of the work being done by the interview team. In addition, Taline accompanied several of the team members to Moscow, where they interviewed Armenians who had emigrated there in search of work; she also went to Stepanakert and did additional interviews related to the war in Nagorno-Karabakh. Korioun Alavardian maintained the database of interviews, arranged transportation for interviewers, maintained a record of hours worked by the interview team, and performed numerous other tasks related to keeping our office functional.

The project was funded by Howard and Roberta Ahmanson through Fieldstead and Company. The Armenian Missionary Association of America (AMAA) served as the fiscal agent for the project, and salaries of project team members were paid through the business office of Haigazian College, supervised by Professor Louis Volpp, president of Haigazian College in Yerevan. With Professor Volpp's assistance, a one-room apartment near his residence was rented as an office for the project. This provided some security for the office contents, which eventually included ten Sanyo tape recorders, four transcribing machines, four laptop computers, a tape-duplicating machine, a fax machine, a camera, one thousand cassette tapes, and a small generator with batteries—all of which were transported from Los Angeles in our luggage.

The project was officially launched in May of 1993, when we hired the research team and did extensive training of the eight interviewers. By the end of August, 232 interviews had been done, and our initial goal was to complete the interviewing phase of the project by the end of October, six months after the interviewing process had begun. In spite of our understanding with the interview team, we did not have the heart to terminate their employment as the winter was approaching. We kept them on and, beginning on January 1, 1994, increased their salaries from $30 a month to $40 a month. While some interviewing continued over the winter months—which was a great supplement to the project—we had most of the research team typing transcripts of interviews.

We did not use these transcripts for translation purposes. Instead, Arpi Haleblian, a resident of California and companion on our trip to Nagorno-Karabakh, volunteered to translate all 289 of the usable interviews (a few of the interview tapes were not legible due to recording and technical problems). She dictated her translation into a tape recorder while listening to each tape, and Angie Martinez, a superb typist, then transcribed these tapes. While a more systematic process of transcription and translation would have been desirable, the cost of transcribing all of the tapes into Armenian and then doing line-by-line translation into English was prohibitive within the boundaries of our budget. Nevertheless, we are confident that the integrity of the meaning of each interview has been maintained.

Under close supervision, our daughter, Arpi Miller, a recent sociology graduate from the University of Southern California, coded all 289 interviews using the QSR Nud*ist program for qualitative analysis. The advantage of this software is that individual sentences or paragraphs can be coded and then retrieved so that one can see the context of a specific quotation. A total of 277 different codes were developed, utilizing three broad categories: (1) comments regarding specific experiences, (2) interpretation and analysis by interviewees of their experiences, and (3) various "free nodes" that allowed for coding comments that did not fit the first two broad categories. Most of the manuscript for this book was written by Donald Miller during a sabbatical leave from the University of Southern California during the fall semester of 2000. The epilogue was written nearly a year later, after a visit to Armenia and Nagorno-Karabakh in April of 2001.

This relatively abstract summary of the methodology for this project does not really capture the experience of conducting the research and the subsequent engagement with the photographic exhibits that traveled the country, as well as the speaking opportunities related to the project and the process of mailing the photoessay to thousands of public officials, opinion makers, and academics. Without doubt, this has been the most complex, demanding, and exhausting project that either of us has undertaken, which probably accounts for the long delay in writing this book, not to mention that we were both holding down our regular fulltime jobs.

The first complications were the distance and the social conditions once we arrived. Getting to Armenia takes several days, and in 1993 it required traveling through Paris and landing in Armenia in the middle of the night. While we lived in the lap of luxury (relatively speaking) in the Hotel Armenia, it was nevertheless somewhat challenging to negotiate power outages, deal with the lack of running water, and so on, although we got used to hanging our camping shower outside on the balcony. Transportation was not a problem, since we were able to pay a driver $10 a day (plus gas) and could go anywhere we wanted. What was most stressful was seeing the living conditions of people. In the four months from May to August 1993, the value of the ruble went from 850 per dollar to 1,400. More disturbing was the weight loss that we could see in people (20–30 pounds for many people over the winter). Although most people dressed well (wearing clothes from more prosperous times), many were clearly struggling with basic survival. The incongruity of this situation in a country with a population of well-educated people was painful, especially every time we returned to supermarkets in southern California.

Other complications arose from adding a visual component to this project. Working with Jerry Berndt was a great enrichment to our lives, and one that has subsequently blossomed into a number of additional projects in the Los Angeles context. What was completely new, however, was creating a catalog of photographs, mounting exhibits (who would have dreamed that Jerry's photographs would be in the rotunda of the Senate Office Building in Washington, D.C.?), and carrying this message to public officials. Through divine providence, we developed a relationship with Margi Denton, who designed the photo-essay and with whom we have subsequently worked on numerous other projects. Equally fortunate was the fact that Charles Hachadourian moved back to Los Angeles from Armenia and worked on every aspect of the traveling exhibit, "Armenia: Portraits of Survival," including overseeing the framing of the photographs, building traveling cases, and mounting the exhibit in various locations. In a one-year period, this exhibit traveled from Los Angeles to Boston, New York, Washington, D.C., Fresno, Pasadena, and Glendale. To our great delight, the Armenian community rallied around the exhibit in each of these locations, producing grand openings for the show and hosting us in wonderful ways. But there was a lot of travel and pressure; we were always worrying about orchestrating the next event. Somehow the refined life of academic reflection had taken a dramatic turn.

The final complication was the writing task itself. Doctoral dissertations are often based on forty to fifty interviews, and here we had almost three hundred—all of which needed to be translated. The sheer mechanics of dealing with thousands of pages of text was a challenge; furthermore, the content was so incredibly depressing. When writing the introduction for the *Survivors* book, we apologized for the delay in publication, saying that it had not been easy to deal with such agonizing material. The same is true of accounts of earthquakes, war, refugees, and starvation.

While we could offer more details about the methodology of this study, perhaps it is appropriate to end with one story. In the summer of 1994 we went to Armenia to pack up the office in Yerevan and bring home the audiotapes. We had left tape recorders and transcribing machines, along with the computers, to be used in Haigazian College. But how were we to carry eight hundred cassette tapes? We decided to pack them into two hardcover suitcases: the original tapes in one suitcase and the copies in the other.

As a precaution, we decided to get a security clearance to avoid any problems at the airport. Several people told us that this could be obtained at a government office in Yerevan, so we went to the appropriate office and waited several hours until an official was willing to see us. He was friendly enough, but said that this was out of his jurisdiction. We needed to go to the airport. So off we trekked to the airport, where we waited and waited, and finally spoke with the head of one of the departments. We explained the project to this official, who said he would have to listen to every one of the tapes to make certain that none of them contained subversive information. Patiently we reiterated that we were leaving tomorrow and that this would be very difficult. Our time problems, however, were of no concern to him. Through a translator we tried every angle, explaining our good intentions, the fact that we had provided employment for the local population, and so on and so on. Finally, out of desperation, we took out a copy of our *Survivors* book and presented it to him as a gift.

It may have been a minor act of God, but this present changed his entire countenance. Within the next few minutes he started telling us the story of his own family, of his wife's illness, and of the difficult time they had experienced during the past winter. To our amazement, he took a Bible off the shelf and started quoting scripture to us, including the passage about Jesus and the tax collector. (Perhaps we had missed the point of his procrastination.) Meanwhile, the tape recorder he had summoned was playing the first of the tapes in the background. He was oblivious to the sound. Instead, a human connection had been made. We ended by hugging each other while a subordinate sealed our suitcases with an official stamp.

Appendix 2

A. Personal Background

1. What is your name? (Ask for maiden name and exact spelling of full name.)

2. What is your address? How long have you lived at this address? (If less than six months, ask for previous address.)

3. What is your telephone number? (if he or she has a telephone)

4. Please give me the name and telephone number of a relative or friend, if I cannot contact you at the above address.

5. Are you married? If so, what is the name of your spouse?

6. Do you have children? If so, what are their names and ages?
   - How many of these children are currently living with you?
   - Do you have any adopted children? (If so, please explain the context of adoption.)
   - Does anyone else live in your household with you (e.g., parents, aunts, uncles, friends)?

7. Are you currently working?
   - If currently working:
     - What is your job? Employer?
     - Are you working full-time? Part-time?

- How long have you been working there?
- Would you mind telling me your approximate salary?
- If not currently working:
  - What was your last job? Employer?
  - When were you employed there?
  - How long were you employed there?
  - What was your approximate salary?
  - Do you currently draw a pension? If so, how much?

8. What is your educational background?
   - Degrees?
   - Name of school(s)?

9. What languages do you speak?
   - List in order of fluency.

10. Where were you born?
    - What year?
    - Other places you have lived?
    - Length of time in each location?

11. Childhood:
    - How many brothers and sisters did you have?
    - Did you live with both parents?
    - What was your father's/mother's occupation?
    - Financially, how comfortable was your childhood?

12. How many members of your extended family—parents, brothers, sisters, aunts, uncles, etc.—live in this city or area?
    - If extended family does not live nearby, where do they live?
      - How often do they communicate with family members?

B. Experience Last Winter

1. How did your family deal with the cold last winter?
   - What was the average temperature in your house on a typical day?
   - What was your source of heat?
   - What did you do to stay warm? Did you sleep in your clothes?
   - How did you cook? Did you eat many of your meals cold? What was your diet like?
   - What was your source of light? How often did you spend evenings in the dark?
   - What problems did you experience getting water? Did you have to carry water? How did you store water?

2. How was your daily routine as a family affected? Describe a typical winter day.
   - Did you stay in your house? Did you visit friends? Were there warm places where you gathered other than your own home? If so, what did you do when you were together as a group?
   - How did your children spend their time?

- How was your routine altered as a result of the cold? How was your spouse's routine changed?

3. If you were not working (or your spouse was not), how demoralizing was it not to have a job? How did you (or your spouse) spend time as a result of not being employed?
   - Did you attempt to educate your children at home while they couldn't go to school? If so, describe this experience.

4. Family relationships:
   - Did the cold result in increased family tensions? Conflicts?
   - Did your family become more close-knit because of the hardship of the cold?

5. In your view, what populations of Armenians were most affected by the cold?
   - Elderly? Refugees? Infants? Children? Men? Women? etc.
   - Those living in cities? Those living in rural areas? Why?
   - Who coped best with the cold?

6. Did you have difficulty getting food last winter?
   - Describe your experience of standing in bread lines. How well did the rationing system work?
   - How was your family's diet different than usual?
   - What was your source of food?
   - Did you receive any food, supplies, or money from relief agencies?
     - What did you receive?
     - How adequate was the assistance?
     - Which relief agencies were most helpful?

7. Did you have any financial problems last winter?
   - What was your source of income?
   - Did friends or relatives help you?
   - Were you able to trade your labor/services for food or other assistance?
   - What is your current source of income?

8. What expressions did you see of people sharing with each other?
   - Did they give each other:
     - Food?
     - Money?
     - Fuel?
     - Other things?
   - Were there any groups of people who seemed to be more generous than others?

9. What do you think will happen next winter?
   - Do you have anxieties about making it through another winter?
   - What specific preparations are you making to cope with another winter if the blockade continues?

C. Emotions

1. How have the blockade and the stresses of the winter months affected you emotionally?

- Have you had any periods of depression?
  - Do you know of other people who seem not to be coping well?
  - How are your children doing?
  - How about your spouse?

2. How did the earthquake affect you emotionally?
   - Did you visit any of the towns affected by the earthquake? If so, what were your emotions at the time?
   - Did the earthquake raise religious questions for you? Did it make you more religious or less religious?
   - In your mind, did you make any connections between the fate of the Armenians during the genocide and the thousands who died during the earthquake?

3. How have you maintained your courage and emotional strength in the face of the economic difficulties caused by the blockade?
   - What have been your sources of emotional strength? (e.g., friends, spouse, children, religion, etc.)

4. How much longer do you think people can live with the blockade?
   - What effect will a continuation of the blockade have on you and on your family?

5. [If unemployed] What effect is continued unemployment having on your emotions and outlook on life?

D. Political Views

1. What are your personal memories of the liberation struggle?
   - Did you participate in demonstrations?
     - What was the purpose of the demonstrations, in your opinion?
     - How large were the crowds?
     - What are some of your most vivid memories from these demonstrations? What do you remember feeling?
   - Describe your feelings when independence was declared in 1991.
     - What celebrations occurred?
     - Were there other events in which you participated?

2. Do you think life is better or worse since Armenia's declaration of independence? In what specific ways?
   - What, if anything, do you miss about the communist system?
   - Are there elements of communism that you would like to see reintroduced into contemporary political life?
   - What do you like about independence?

3. Nagorno-Karabakh:
   - Do you support the liberation movement in Nagorno-Karabakh? Please explain your views.
   - What role do you think the government of Armenia should have in the liberation struggle?

- Have any of your children, friends, or relatives been directly involved in the liberation struggle? Have any been killed?
- What are your political views regarding settling the political conflict with Azerbaijan?
  - Do you favor some form of political compromise? If so, what form would that compromise take?

4. How have each of the following contributed to the current political and economic difficulties in Armenia?
   - The current political leadership
   - Tashnags
   - Russians
   - Turks
   - Azeris
   - Americans

5. How successfully have the following populations of refugees been integrated into Armenian society, and what should the government be doing to assist these different groups of people?
   - Refugees from Baku and Sumgait
   - Refugees from Nagorno-Karabakh
   - People displaced by the 1988 earthquake

6. With regard to the refugees, have they been able to find jobs? What is their housing situation?
   - Are these different populations of refugees resented by most Armenians?
   - Do you resent them?
   - Are they viewed as a burden on the government?

7. How has your life been affected by the blockade?
   - Employment
   - Transportation
   - Medical care
   - Household commodities
   - Education
   - Recreation
   - Cultural events
   - Public services

8. What populations of people have been most affected by the blockade? What groups of people have been least affected?
   - Have any family members or close friends died as a direct result of the blockade?
   - What do you think are the reasons for the blockade, and what needs to happen for the blockade to be ended?

9. How optimistic are you about the future of Armenia?
   - What hope do you have regarding the potential of Armenia becoming energy self-sufficient by drilling for oil and natural gas?
   - Do you think it was a mistake to shut down the nuclear power plant?

- How optimistic are you that Nagorno-Karabakh will remain independent?
- How long do you think Armenia will be involved in war and political conflict?
- Do you think the blockade will end soon?
- If the blockade continues through next winter, what will the consequences be for the people of Armenia?
- How do you feel about your children's future?

E. Earthquake Survivors

1. Please describe what you experienced on December 7, 1988, and during the days immediately thereafter.

2. Did you lose family members/friends during the earthquake?
   - Please identify how many, and their relationship to you.
   - How were they killed or injured?

3. Was your home destroyed by the earthquake? If so, where are you currently living?
   - Describe your current living situation. Where else did you live after your house was destroyed?
   - Has there been any reconstruction of your home? Place of work? Schools? Public facilities?

4. Please describe your feelings of loss as a result of the earthquake. How has this experience affected you emotionally?
   - Do you find yourself frequently thinking about the earthquake?
   - How fearful are you of another earthquake?
   - How frequently are you depressed?
   - How do you try to cope with your feelings of loss and depression?

5. What have been your sources of emotional and physical strength since the earthquake?
   - Church? Religion?
   - Family?
   - Friends?

6. How has your life changed as a result of the earthquake?
   - The lives of your children?
   - Your spouse?
   - Your relatives?

7. How hopeful are you that things can ever return to normal—to the way they were prior to the earthquake?
   - What currently gives you hope for the future?
   - What do you find most discouraging about your life situation?

8. Do you think relief aid was effectively used?
   - What relief assistance did you personally receive?
   - In your town, what relief assistance was most helpful?
   - Did you see relief assistance being wasted?

. Do you think that there was much fraud related to money given for relief efforts? If so, by what groups? Please give specific examples.
- What groups were most efficient in their use of relief funds?

9. Immediately after the earthquake there were a lot of theories about the
source of the earthquake, including the possibility that it was a result of
underground nuclear bomb tests conducted by the Soviet government.
- Did you believe any of these theories? Do you still? Or do you think
that it was simply a natural disaster?

10. Have you wondered why God allowed the earthquake to occur?
- Do you think God had anything to do with the earthquake?
- How has your faith changed as a result of the earthquake? Is it stronger
or weaker?

F. Refugees from Azerbaijan

1. How would you describe the relations between Armenians and Azeris
before the massacres in Baku and Sumgait?
- Did Armenians and Azeris live together in the same neighborhoods?
- Did they intermarry?
- Did Armenian and Azeri children play together? Did parents socialize
together?

2. Please describe the circumstances that forced you to leave Azerbaijan.
- Did you observe any political violence against your family? Other
Armenians?
- Describe as specifically as possible what you observed.
- Were any of your family members or friends killed, tortured, or threat-
ened?

3. Describe your trip to Armenia.
- What were you able to bring with you?
- What did you leave behind?
- What hardships did you experience coming to Armenia?
- Did you get separated from anyone in your immediate family?

4. Where did you live when you first arrived in Armenia?
- Describe your first few weeks.
- How many different places have you lived in Armenia?

5. Have you found it difficult to become integrated into Armenian society?
- Did you know Armenians before arriving here?
- What difficulties have your children or spouse experienced in adjusting
to Armenian society?
- Do you think that your chances of succeeding in Armenia are different
from those of Armenians who were born here?
- Do you feel resentment from Armenians who were born here?
- Do you think that the blockade has affected you and your family more
than it did Armenians who were born here?

6. Has the government provided you with assistance?

- How adequate has it been?
- What form has it taken? Housing? Money?

7. Describe your current situation:
   - Where are you living?
   - Are you working? If not, what are your chances of obtaining work?
   - How are your children doing?
   - Are they happy?
   - How are they doing in school?

8. Do you have any desire to return to Azerbaijan?
   - Does your spouse want to return?
   - Do your children?
   - What do you miss most about your life in Azerbaijan?
   - Have any of your friends who came to Armenia emigrated to other places? (e.g., Russia)

9. How hopeful are you about the future?
   - What gives you hope about your future?
   - What discourages you?

G. Women

1. If your husband is not working, how has this changed family life?
   - Are men more helpful with household chores?
   - Have the socioeconomic consequences of the blockade affected your relationship with your spouse? If so, how?
   - Do you find men to be more or less demanding?
   - Do you find your husband to be more or less accommodating to family needs?
   - Do you think that there has been an increase or decrease in the level of family violence? Abuse of children? Women?

2. Do you think more women or men have lost their jobs as a result of the blockade?
   - Have men or women had more difficulty coping with the economic problems caused by the blockade?

3. What ingenious methods have you developed to deal with preserving food and fuel as a result of the blockade?
   - What other innovations have occurred in household life? (e.g., related to water, bathing, etc.)

4. Is the blockade affecting any of the following?
   - The number of women seeking education
   - The number of women having abortions
   - The number of couples getting married

5. How have you observed neighbors helping each other as a result of the blockade?

6. Who has been most helpful to you in dealing with the stresses and strains of the blockade?

H. Religion

1. Since political independence, do you think people are more or less religious?
   - How has your faith changed?
   - Do you go to church more or less frequently?
   - Do you think there has been an increase in the number of people being married in the church? Buried?
   - Are more children being baptized?

2. What church, if any, do you attend?
   - Do you believe in God? What does it mean to you to believe in God?
   - In a typical month, how often do you attend worship services?
   - How important is religion to you? Your spouse? Your children?
   - Do you regularly read the Bible or engage in any daily religious practice?
   - Have you had any type of religious conversion experience?

3. How helpful has the church been in meeting people's spiritual, emotional, and physical needs?
   - In offering comfort?
   - In interpreting why the earthquake happened?
   - In giving relief assistance?

Appendix 3

Interviewees

Individuals who wished to remain anonymous are not included in this list.

Angela Abrahamian
Anna Abrahamian
Bella Abramian
Hrant Adamian
Silva Adamian
Genrikh Agabekov
Rafik Aganov
Armen Aivazian
Dekhtsanik Aivazian
Lourence Aivazian
Naira Aivazian
Volodia Aivazian
Helena Alakhverdian
Albert Alaverdian
Aida Aleksanian
Andranik Aleksanian
Robert Alexanian
Albert Alikhanian

Inga Amirian
Natalia Amirian
Genadi Amirjanian
Ghenia Anastasian
Lelly Andreasian
Nazeli Antablian
Onik Antablian
Mnatsakan Antikian
Artashes Antonov
Gagik Arakelian
Larisa Arakelova
Valia Arakelova
Helena Arushanian
Samvel Arushanian
Armine Arustamian
Aram Asatrian
Naira Asatrian
Seda Asatrian

Vardan Asatrian
Alexander Aslanian
Arzik Asrian
Leonid Atoyan
Alisa Avakian
Nelly Avakian
Anna Avanesian
Emilia Avanesian
Anahit Avdalian
Amalia Avetisian
Ashot Avetisian
Margarit Avetisian
Nina Avetisian
Varinka Avetisian
Kristine Ayvazian
Hamaspoor Azizian
Lilit Aznawurian
Eduard Babayan

Nelly Babayan
Mr. Babken
Arev Baghdasarian
Armen Baghdasarian
Larisa Baghdasarian
Mr. Bagoyan
Mkrtich Balagiozian
Boris Barsamian
Pavel Barseghian
Arthur Barsegian
Hamest Beglarian
Nora Beglarian
Avetis Berberian
Susanna Boshtolian
Susanna Broian
Piruza Brutian
Grigori Chalabian
Gohar Chaljian
Diana Chilingarian
Rhonda Cooper
Ashot Douloyan
Viacheslav Danielian
Tamara Dashian
Liuba Davoyan
Evelina Djantchian
Elizavetya Egiazarian
Tonik Elbakian
Vanik Elizbarian
Armen Erian
Agrafena Eritsian
Anaheet Ezekian
Anna Ezekian
Armen Falajian
Marat Farajian
Vladimir Gabrielov
Levon Galustian
Benic Gasparian
Geghetsik Gasparian
Margarita Gasparian
Alla Gevorgian
Emma Gevorkian
Sofia Gevorkian
Stasia Gevorkian
Tsolak Gevorkian
Naira Ghaitanjian
Levon Gharibian
Kostansia Ghasabian

Ruzanna Ghazarian
Arkadi Giulzadian
Nelson Gjaguntz
Edvin Grigorian
Gagik Grigorian
Igor Grigorian
Knarik Grigorian
Naira Grigorian
Nelly Grigorian
Petia Grigorian
Rosa Grigorian
Samvel Grigorian
Valeri Grigorian
Nektar Hagian
Vshtuni Hajkian
Hratch Hakhumian
Horom Hakopian
Ira Hakopian
Karine Hakopian
Suzanna Hakopian
Naira Haroyan
Andranik Harutiunian
Arpig Harutiunian
Gayane Harutiunian
Irana Harutiunian
Lusine Harutiunian
Natalia Harutiunian
Shura Harutiunian
Srpuhi Harutiunian
Maria Harutunian
Margarita Hayrapetian
David Heemsberger
Varouzhan Hogtanian
Samvel Hovakimian
Hamazasp Hovanesian
Hovanes Hovanesian
Volodia Hovanesian
Tigran Hovanessian
Vitali Hovhanissian
Asot Hovhannisian
Flora Hovhannisian
Naira Hovhannisian
Razmik Hovhannisian
Vergine Hovhannisian
Vilena Hovhannisian
Artak Hovsepian
Henrik Hovsepian

Hrant Isagulian
Yura Ispandarian
Evgenia Israelian
Henrik Israelian
Aida Jianshian
Naira Karakhanian
Atom Karapetian
Gohar Karapetian
Varduhi Karapetian
Gohar Khachatrian
Margo Khachatrian
Rafael Khachatrian
Rouzanna Khachatrian
Vardishar Khachatrian
Samvel Khalachian
Lilia Khalapian
Manvel Kharatian
Mila Kharatian
Ashot Khazarian
Varsenik Khazarian
Tamara Khlkhadjian
Gurgen Khnkoyan
Tereza Khnorian
Grigor Khoshorian
Liudmila Khukasian
Hrach Kilikian
Hajkanush Kirakosian
Silva Kirakosova
Hamlet Kiurerian
Valentina Krivaruchko
Eduard Longurian
Smbat Madatian
Angela Malitvina
Asia Malkhasian
Lamara Mangasarian
Armen Manoukian
Zakar Manoukian
Ruben Manucharian
Hovsep Manukian
Mary Manukian
Sos Manukian
Robert Mardoyan
Eduard Martirosian
Martiros Martirosian
Rafic Martirosian
Zhora Martirosian
Erzhinka Matevosian

Ashot Melian
Hasmik Melikian
Pavel Melikian
Samvel Melikian
Takuhi Meliksetian
Arpig Melkonian
Arsen Melkonian
Genia Melkumian
Irina Melkumian
Nelly Melkumian
Anahit Merzoyan
Liuda Mezhlumian
Gurgen Mikaelian
Hambartsum
   Mikaelian
Julietta Mikaelian
Shoghakat Militosian
Ashot Minasian
Suren Mirabian
Knarik Mirzoyan
Sergei Misakian
Armen Mkrtchian
Larisa Mkrtchian
Zhanna Mkrtchian
Aida Movsesian
Dianna Nazaretian
Liudmila Nazarian
Hayk Nersesian
Karina Nersesian
Armen Nersisian
Varsik Nikoyan
Arthur Oganesian
Grigor Ohanian
Tonia Ohanian
Ruzanna Ordian
Nina Parsian
Hratch Periverdian
Gohar Petrosian

Liuba Petrosian
Suren Petrosian
Gayane Piliposian
Arshaluis Poghosian
Gricor Revinian
Armen Rostomian
Varia Sagian
Arevhat Sahakian
Arsen Sahakian
Lianna Sahakian
Zarik Sahakian
Anna Sardarian
Karine Sardarian
Ashot Sargsian
Nazeli Sargsian
Shushanik Sargsian
Virab Sargsian
Margaret Sarkisian
Mark Sarkisian
Nazeli Sarkisian
Valia Sarkisian
Ashot Saroyan
Alexander Sarukhanian
Rafael Seiranian
Gayane Setrakian
Haikanush Setrakian
Narine Shahbasian
Nelly Shahinian
Kima Shahvazian
Hrachik Shakhbazian
Sergei Shakhparonian
Alexander Shirinian
Zara Shirinian
Anaheet Simonian
Arthur Simonian
Karine Simonian
Narine Smbatian
Silva Soromonian

Alexander Talalian
Rakhilia Tamasian
Rima Tatevosian
Harutiun Tatylian
Artiom Ter-Budaghian
Roland Ter-Hovanesian
Marina Ter-Hovsepian
Seda Ter-Sahakian
Yuri Ter-Stepanian
Norik Tevonian
Rafael Tigranian
Garbis Titizian
Nikola Tjagharian
Anaheet Torosian
Vachik Torosian
Artavazd Tosunian
Sopha Tovmasova
Sona Tumanian
Roza Vanian
Albert Vardanian
Alina Vardanian
Armen Vardanian
Armen Vardanian
Norik Vardanian
Volodia Varosian
Gayane Vasilian
Knarik Voskanian
Julietta Yarazian
Seiran Yarmourian
Stepan Yeritsian
Anaheet Zagarian
Anna Zakarian
Anahit Zakoyan
Armenuhi Zamanian
Asia Zargarian
Sarkis Zavarian

Bibliography

Abrahamyan, Levon H. "The Karabagh Movement as Viewed by an Anthropologist." *Armenian Review* 43, no. 2–3 (summer/autumn 1990): 67–80.

Adalian, Rouben P. *Armenia and Karabagh Factbook.* Washington, D.C.: Armenian Assembly of America, 1996.

AIM Staff. "Got Tanks, Will Travel." *AIM* 4, no. 4 (April/May 1993): 16–20.

Altstadt, Audrey L. *The Azerbaijani Turks: Power and Identity under Russian Rule.* Stanford, CA: Hoover Institution Press, 1992.

Arlen, Michael J. *Passage to Ararat.* New York: Farrar, Straus & Giroux, 1975.

Armenian Assembly <*http://www.aaainc.org/*>. Position papers and archived news related to the Republic of Armenia and Karabakh are available on this website.

Armenian National Committee <*http://www.anca.org/anca/*>. Position papers on various issues related to the Republic of Armenia and Karabakh are available on this website.

Astourian, Stepan H. "On the Rise of Azerbaijani National Identity and Armeno-Azerbaijani Relations." *Armenian Review* 40, no. 3 (fall 1987): 33–45.

Burg, Steven L. "Nationality Elites and Political Change in the Soviet Union." In *The Nationalities Factor in Soviet Politics and Society,* ed. Lubomyr Hajda and Mark Beissinger. Boulder, CO: Westview Press, 1990.

Chaliand, Gerard, and Yves Ternon. *The Armenians: From Genocide to Resistance.* Tr. Tony Berret. London: Zed Press, 1983.

Chalk, Frank, and Kurt Jonassohn. *The History and Sociology of Genocide: Analyses and Case Studies.* New Haven, CT: Yale University Press, 1990.

Chandler, Andrea, and Charles F. Futado Jr., eds. *Perestroika in the Soviet Republics: Documents on the National Question.* Boulder, CO: Westview Press, 1992.

Charny, Israel. *How Can We Commit the Unthinkable? Genocide: The Human Cancer.* Boulder, CO: Westview Press, 1982.

Chorbajian, Levon. *Karabakh and the U.S. Press: A Study in Mythmaking.* Cambridge, MA: Zoryan Institute, 1988.

Chorbajian, Levon, Patrick Donabedian, and Claude Mutafian. *The Caucasian Knot: The History and Geo-Politics of Nagorno-Karabagh.* London and Atlantic Highlands, NJ: Zed Books, 1994.

Cox, Caroline, and John Eibner. *Ethnic Cleansing in Progress: War in Nagorno Karabakh.* Zurich, London, and Washington, D.C.: Institute for Religious Minorities in the Islamic World, 1993.

Dekmejian, R. Hrair. "Determinants of Genocide: Armenians and Jews as Case Studies." In *The Armenian Genocide in Perspective,* ed. Richard G. Hovannisian. New Brunswick: Transaction Books, 1986.

Dragadze, Tamara. "The Armenian-Azerbaijani Conflict: Structure and Sentiment." *Third World Quarterly* 11, no. 1 (January 1989).

Dudwick, Nora. "The Karabagh Movement: An Old Scenario Gets Rewritten." *Armenian Review* 42, no. 3 (autumn 1989).

Fein, Helen. *Accounting for Genocide: National Responses and Jewish Victimization During the Holocaust.* New York: Free Press, 1979.

Frelick, Bill. *Faultlines of Nationality Conflict: Refugees and Displaced Persons from Armenia and Azerbaijan.* Washington, D.C.: The U.S. Committee for Refugees.

Goldenberg, Suzanne. *Pride of Small Nations: The Caucasus and Post-Soviet Disorder.* London and Atlantic Highlands, NJ: Zed Books, 1994.

Government of Armenia, UNICEF, and Save the Children, 1998. *Situation Analysis of Children and Women in Armenia: 1998.* Published by UNICEF.

GROONG <*http://groong.usc.edu/*>. Information on Armenia is published daily at this website.

Guroian, Vigen. "Collective Responsibility and Official Excuse Making: The Case of the Turkish Genocide of the Armenians." In *The Armenian Genocide in Perspective,* ed. Richard G. Hovannisian. New Brunswick, NJ: Transaction Books, 1986.

Halpin, Tony, and Gayane Mkrtchian. "Faith Forward." *AIM* 12, no. 8 (October 2001): 28–38.

Herzig, Edmund M. "Armenians." In *The Nationalities Question in the Soviet Union.* Ed. Graham Smith. London: Longman, 1990.

Hovannisian, Raffi. *Nagorno Karabagh: A White Paper.* Washington, D.C.: Armenian Assembly of America, 1997.

Hovannisian, Richard G. *Armenia on the Road to Independence: 1918.* Berkeley and Los Angeles: University of California Press, 1967.

———. "The Armeno-Azerbaijani Conflict over Mountainous Karabagh, 1918–1919." *Armenian Review* 24, no. 2 (summer 1971): 3–39.

———. *The Republic of Armenia.* Vol. 1. *The First Year, 1918–1919.* Berkeley and Los Angeles: University of California Press, 1971.

———. *The Republic of Armenia.* Vol. 2. *From Versailles to London, 1919–1920.* Berkeley and Los Angeles: University of California Press, 1971.

———. "Nationalist Ferment in Armenia." In *Freedom at Issue* no. 105 (November/December 1988): 29–35.

———, ed. *The Armenian Genocide in Perspective.* New Brunswick, NJ: Transaction Books, 1986.

———, ed. *The Armenian Genocide: History, Politics, Ethics.* New York: St. Martin's Press, 1992.

Hratch Tchilingirian, "From Activism to Diplomacy." *AIM* 10, no. 4 (April 1999): 34–39.

Human Development Report, Armenia 1999: Five Years of Human Development in Armenia. United Nations Development Program, 1999.

Human Rights and Human Development: Action for Progress. Armenia 2000. United Nations Development Program, 2000.

Karanian, Matthew. "Earthquake '88: The Rebuilding Continues." *AIM* 10, no.1 (January 1999): 22–25.

———. "Power to the People." *AIM* 11, no. 8–9 (August/September 2000): 60–69.

Kuper, Leo. *Genocide: Its Political Use in the Twentieth Century.* New Haven, CT: Yale University Press, 1982.

———. *The Prevention of Genocide.* New Haven, CT: Yale University Press, 1985.

Laitin, David D., and Robert Grigor Suny. "Armenia and Azerbaijan: Thinking a Way Out of Karabakh." *Middle East Policy* 7, no. 1 (October 1999): 145–76.

Lang, David Marshall. *Armenia: Cradle of Civilization.* London: George Allen & Unwin, 1970.

Libaridian, Gerard J. *The Karabagh File: Documents and Facts on the Question of Mountainous Karabagh, 1918–1988.* Cambridge, MA, and Toronto: The Zoryan Institute, 1988.

———. *Armenia at the Crossroads: Democracy and Nationhood in the Post-Soviet Era.* Watertown, MA: Blue Crane Books, 1991.

Malkasian, Mark. *Gha-ra-bagh: The Emergence of the National Democratic Movement in Armenia.* Detroit, MI: Wayne State University Press, 1996.

Melson, Robert. "A Theoretical Inquiry into the Armenian Massacres of 1894–96." *Comparative Studies in Society and History* 24 (1982): 481–509.

———. "Provocation or Nationalism: A Critical Inquiry into the Armenian Genocide of 1915." In *The Armenian Genocide in Perspective,* edited by Richard G. Hovannisian, 61–84. New Brunswick: Transaction Books, 1986.

Miller, Donald E., and Lorna Touryan Miller. "Armenian Survivors: A Typological Analysis of Victim Response." *Oral History Review* 10 (1982): 47–72.

———. "Memory and Identity across the Generations: A Case Study of Armenian Survivors and Their Progeny." *Qualitative Sociology* 14 (1991): 13–38.

———. *Survivors: An Oral History of the Armenian Genocide.* Berkeley and Los Angeles: University of California Press, 1993.

Mirak, Robert. "Armenians." In *Harvard Encyclopedia of American Ethnic Groups,* ed. Stephan Thernstrom. Cambridge, MA: Harvard University Press, 1980.

Monthly Digest of News from Armenia. Office of Research and Analysis. Washington, D.C.: Armenian Assembly. Issued monthly in 1993/94.

Mouradian, Claire. "Caricature in the Armenian Press of the Caucacas." *Armenian Review* 44, no. 1 (winter 1991): 1–35.

"Nagorno-Karabagh Crisis: A Blueprint for Resolution." A memorandum prepared by the Public International Law and Policy Group and the New England Center for International Law and Policy, June 2000.

Nahaylo, Bohdan, and Victor Swoboda. *Soviet Disunion: A History of Nationalities Problems in the USSR.* New York: Free Press, 1990.

Nalbandian, Louise. *The Armenian Revolutionary Movement: The Development of Armenian Political Parties through the Nineteenth Century.* Berkeley and Los Angeles: University of California Press, 1963.

Poverty of Vulnerable Groups in Armenia. United Nations Office in Armenia, 1999.

Rutland, Peter. "Democracy and Nationalism in Armenia." *Europe-Asia Studies* 46, no. 5 (September 1994): 839–62.

Sarkissian, Hrair Sarkis. "Thinking Long-Term." *AIM* 12, no. 5 (June 2001): 22–26.

Satamian, Tallitu. "Inching toward the Round Table." *AIM* 4, no. 4 (April/May 1993): 20–21.

Shahmuratian, Samuel, ed. *The Sumgait Tragedy: Pogroms against Armenians in Soviet Azerbaijan.* Vol. 1. *Eyewitness Accounts.* New Rochelle, NY: Aristide D. Caratzas, 1990.

Smith, Roger W. "Human Destructiveness and Politics: The Twentieth Century as an Age of Genocide." In *Genocide and the Modern Age: Etiology and Case Studies of Mass Death,* ed. Isidor Walliman and Michael N. Doblowski. New York: Greenwood Press, 1987.

———. "Genocide and Denial: The Armenian Case and Its Implications." *Armenian Review* 42, no. 1 (spring 1989): 1–38.

Staub, Ervin. *The Roots of Evil: The Origins of Genocide and Other Group Violence.* Cambridge: Cambridge University Press, 1989.

Suny, Ronald. *Looking toward Ararat: Armenia in Modern History.* Bloomington: Indiana University Press, 1993.

Toroyan, Aline. "Shattered House." *AIM* 4, no. 4 (April/May 1993): 23–24.

Toynbee, Arnold. *Armenian Atrocities: The Murder of a Nation.* London: Hodder & Stoughton, 1915.

Verluise, Pierre. *Armenia in Crisis: The 1988 Earthquake.* Tr. Levon Chorbajian. Detroit, MI: Wayne State University Press, 1989.

Walker, Christopher J. *Armenia: The Survival of a Nation.* London: Croom Helm, 1980.

———. *Armenia and Karabagh: The Struggle for Unity.* London: Minority Rights Publications, 1991.

Werfel, Franz. *The Forty Days of Musa Dagh.* New York: Viking Press, 1934.

World Bank. "Republic of Armenia: Interim Poverty Reduction Strategy Paper." March 2001.

Index

Designer: Nola Burger
Compositor: Integrated Composition Systems
Text: 10/13 Sabon
Display: Tasse; Univers Condensed
Printer and Binder: Edwards Brothers, Inc.
Indexer: Andrew Joron